15 Easy Techniques to Strengthen Your Mind, Master Emotional Regulation, Embrace Self-Acceptance to Step Into Your New and Happy Life

HAPPINESS RETURNS

THE SELF-CARE AND SELF-COMPASSION WORKBOOK

ROBERT J. CHARLES, PHD, DMIN

Happiness Returns: The Self-Care and Self-Compassion Workbook

15 Easy Techniques to Strengthen Your Mind, Master Emotional Regulation, Embrace Self-Acceptance to Step Into Your New and Happy Life

By Robert J. Charles, PhD, DMin

Contents

Amazing BONUS!
Companion Worksheets

Embark on a Personal Journey Toward Happiness

7 Transformative Worksheets for Cultivating a New Mindset for a Better Life - For Beginners

Inside this BONUS you'll discover:

- How to Cultivate Self-Compassion for True Happiness?
- How to Unleash Your Happy Hormones?
- How to Create Your ideal Self-Care Routine?

If you want to start a better with self-compassion and self-care

Download this BONUS

Second BONUS

WANT TO OVERCOME OVERTHINKING and MANAGE DIFFICULT PEOPLE?

These **4 FREE** offers are perfect for you: 2 eBooks + 2 audiobooks
<< Click here to discover the consequences of overthinking and how to approach difficult people >>

In these 2 eBooks + 2 audiobooks, YOU will discover:

- The three different forms of overthinking and how to spot them.
- How ruminating and worrying can damage your social life.
- The types of toxic people and how to escape their web of crises.
- How to discover if you are a highly sensitive person and ways to deal with that.

If you want to finally stop overthinking and being manipulated by others…

Click here to get these 4 FREE offers.

"I'm back! What did I miss?..."

Introduction

What can you expect from a group of people caught in the crossfire of what started as a cry for justice but soon descended into a full-blown civil war—people whose families were torn apart and their homes reduced to rubble, their nation in ruins and their lives forever changed?

Happiness? I doubt that…

Yamen is one of the young people caught in the crossfire in Syria and is now a refugee who has faced enormous challenges after arriving in the United States.

With little knowledge of the English language, Yamen took it upon himself to learn. He pored over books, listened to podcasts, and practiced speaking with anyone who would lend an ear. His dedication paid off, and he passed his GED, thanks to the support of a nonprofit school for refugee children.

Yamen's commitment didn't stop there. He began volunteering at the very same school that helped him on his educational journey. Through his tireless efforts, he gained a reputation as a reliable and helpful worker. And then, by a stroke of luck, an incredible donor decided to sponsor him for college.

Curious about how Yamen had managed to find happiness amidst these stark realities, Hugo Huijer (2020), founder of the blog Tracking Happiness, asked him for his secret. His answer was amazingly profound. Yamen said with a smile,

"Happiness is about how you're raised to view things."

Yamen went on to say that despite their struggles, his parents instilled in him and his siblings the belief that they had everything they needed to be happy and taught them to find satisfaction in what they had, rather than yearning for what they lacked. It was a mindset that carried Yamen through times of crisis and uncertainty.

He explained that even now, in the midst of upheaval and challenges, he strives to focus on the present and embrace what he does have—not to dwell on the elusive possibilities of the future, but rather to find contentment in the here and now.

In an age where so many things, including our daily lives, are defined by social media, we often find ourselves striving for happiness, seeking fulfillment in external accomplishments and possessions. However, true happiness isn't something we can find outside of ourselves. It resides within us, waiting to be discovered and nurtured.

This book, *Happiness Returns: The Self-Compassion and Self-Care Workbook*, is a guide that will lead you towards unlocking the secrets to a truly contented and fulfilling life.

Each chapter is a treasure chest that takes you deeper into the core of your being—meaning, we're not necessarily embarking on a utopic journey to a fabulous future, where all things are perfect; rather, we're diving deep into the depths of our being, exploring the profound connection between self-compassion, self-care, emotional wellbeing, and happiness.

This journey begins in Chapter 1, where we lay the foundation by understanding the essence of self-compassion. We explore the transformative power of being kind to oneself, fostering a gentle and understanding relationship with our inner selves. This leads us to discover that self-compassion is not only an act of kindness but also a catalyst for personal growth and happiness.

Taking a step further, we explore the fascinating world of happiness in Chapter 2. We're not just talking about the superficial experience here; we're diving into the psychology behind it all. We want to understand what truly makes us happy—is it just a temporary mood or something more profound? We'll debunk some common misconceptions and unravel the key elements that contribute to a deep sense of joy. By delving into the intricacies of happiness, we'll equip ourselves with the knowledge and insights to create a life that's brimming with authentic contentment.

With the wisdom of self-compassion and a solid understanding of true happiness, Chapter 3 introduces us to the practice of mindful self-compassion. This mindfulness helps us approach ourselves with kindness and understanding. By embracing mindful self-compassion, we're setting ourselves on a powerful path towards happiness. It's a journey that nurtures our wellbeing in the present moment, embraces our imperfections, and fosters personal growth.

In Chapter 4, we'll explore the intriguing connection between self-esteem and happiness. There's a complex dance between these two forces, and we want to understand how having a healthy sense of self-worth can impact our overall wellbeing and long-term happiness. There are proven practices that can boost our self-esteem and empower us to lead lives filled with confidence, authenticity, and a genuine appreciation for who we truly are.

Emotional health plays a vital role in our pursuit of happiness, and that's exactly what Chapter 5 is all about. We're going to explore strategies to nurture our emotional wellbeing, enhance our resilience, and cultivate positive emotions. Life throws challenges our way, but by mastering the skills of emotional wellbeing, we'll have the tools to stay in a happy state even when the going gets tough.

Chapter 6 tackles a common roadblock on our path to happiness: depression. Depression is often one of the reasons for the loss of amazing souls in our communities. It isn't a plague against one person, but against an entire race. And it doesn't respect status, background, color, or tongue. Therefore, it's important to deal with the plague of depression before it robs us of our brightest minds.

In Chapter 7, we're all about strengthening our minds. Your mind is the center of the action. That's what this whole book is targeting. It's also the place from which negativity emanates, if we let it. To have a negative mentality is to be toxic and pessimistic and not even try to live happily. This chapter, therefore, aims at reprogramming our mentality to discover the incredible inner strength within each of us. We'll share practical techniques to cultivate a resilient mindset. With these tools, we can face adversity with courage and come out stronger on the other side.

The last chapter, Chapter 8, brings us to the crucial pillar of self-care. We'll uncover the transformative impact of nourishing our minds, bodies, and spirits. This chapter reveals the practices and rituals that promote a happier and more fulfilling existence. By embracing self-care as an integral part of our lives, we'll create a solid foundation for sustained happiness, ensuring that our wellbeing remains a top priority.

As you embark on this incredible internal journey through the pages of *The Self-Compassion and Self-Care Workbook*, always remember that true happiness isn't some far-off destination—it's a way of being and living. By embracing self-compassion and self-care, and by understanding the psychology of happiness, you will give yourself the power to transform your life and experience the joy that you deserve.

Don't try to rush to finish this book as quickly as possible. I recommend you take each chapter a week at a time, or read one part over the span of a week, whichever one works for you. Just ensure you get the most from these pages.

So, let's embark on this transformative adventure together and cultivate a life filled with happiness, purpose, and a deep love for ourselves.

I'm ready whenever you're ready to flip to the next page.

Robert

PART 1

Self-Compassion and Its Link to Happiness

Happiness is abstract, and it means different things to different people.

As abstract as it is, though, virtually everyone is in search of happiness. Everyone wants a share of it. Our search for happiness takes us to different places. Unfortunately, many people are usually frustrated and met with disappointment when they don't find happiness in the places their search takes them.

So, where does happiness reside? How can you possibly handle something as abstract as happiness?

As I guide you through the first part of this book, you'll realize that what we seek isn't lost. Happiness is naturally attracted to another abstract phenomenon: love. So, to be happy, you need to understand love first. And before anything or anyone else, you need to be able to love yourself.

In this part, you'll also learn that happiness goes beyond superficial appearances. There's a psychological dimension to it. The objective of this part is to help you see and understand that dimension so that you won't be tossed about by transient emotional outbursts.

Are you ready for a mental paradigm shift? Then this is for you. Let's get started.

CHAPTER 1

Being Kind to Self

"Love your neighbor as yourself."

—Matthew 19:19

"Be nice to yourself… It's hard to be happy when someone is mean to you all the time."

—Christine Arylo

During my undergrad studies, I had an amazing friend named Maya. She was a sweet young woman, the kind you always love to have in your circle. She always put everyone else's needs before her own. She was a loving and supportive friend who went above and beyond to make sure everyone around her was happy and taken care of.

However, amidst all her selflessness, I noticed that Maya wasn't giving herself as much care as she gave to others. In fact, she rarely took time for self-care and would dismiss her own needs and desires, believing that they were not as important as those of others. Over time, this self-neglect started taking a toll on her wellbeing. She felt drained, overwhelmed, and constantly stressed.

Although it took time for her to reevaluate her priorities, she eventually had a moment of realization. She began to realize that in order to be truly there for others and make a positive impact, she needed to start being kind to herself as well. She had always thought it was selfish to look out for herself, but now she knows better. Looking out for herself was the realest act of self-compassion and self-preservation.

As a step toward reinventing herself and living a truly happy life, Maya told me then that she now sets aside some time each day just for herself. She admitted that there was a limit to what she could do for people. This helped her learn how to set boundaries. Of course, these changes didn't happen as swiftly as waving a magic wand. It took some time for her to make these adjustments. But in those moments of transformation, she evolved into a happier friend.

—*Olivia*

Taking a cue from Maya's story, I'd consider this the golden rule for being truly happy in life: love yourself first.

"Hey, don't give me that look!"

Self-Compassion: Crucial to Happiness

Does anyone deserve to be happier than you?

I can imagine your hesitation in responding to that question. Your piety and generous mind kicked in the moment you read that question because you want people around you to be happy too—even happier than you are, perhaps. Well, I don't dispute that. Every well-meaning person deserves to be happy.

But should they be happier at your expense?

Do you deserve to be happy?

Those questions are not intended to undermine your intention to do the things you do for other people; rather, they're intended to make you reflect—an introspective reflection of your actions, ideals, and perspectives in relation to your total wellbeing.

You, my reader, are the focus of this book, not the other person you care so much about (although you can recommend the book to them as well, and I encourage you to do so). But at this moment, I see you alone. And you are the focus of my long hours at my writing desk.

Self-compassion is crucial to your happiness, yes! But who is this self, and why does it need compassion?

Using *self* as an affix is pretty common today. Because of this, many people use *self-this* and *self-that* casually without thinking about what "self" actually means. I'm telling you right now, "self" is not just a word. It is a reference to a living entity.

Let's take a quick look at ***what or who this self is.*** I'm going to be a bit analytical in trying to help you understand the self.

The ancient Greek philosopher Aristotle believed that when it comes to the self, it's all about the combination of the body and soul. He called this idea "hylomorphic." Basically, you can't separate the two—they're always connected. So, talking about the self means considering both the body and the soul. Aristotle believed that the self is essentially a harmonious blend of the physical and immaterial aspects (Admin, 2022).

In summary, according to Aristotle, the self is a combination of the body and the soul. This is the first point.

Another philosopher whose perspective I'd like us to consider is Socrates. I love his view on this. Socrates had a different take on the true self. He didn't think it was about what we owned, our social status, our reputation, or even our physical bodies. According to Socrates, our true self is actually our soul. This means that the essence of who we really are goes beyond material possessions or external factors. Socrates became famous for emphasizing the importance of our inner being, our soul, as the core of our true selves (Academy of Ideas, 2015).

On this point, Socrates and Aristotle seemed to agree about the soul being the true self.

Do you have a soul?

Two more definitions, and then you'll see what I'm trying to paint vividly.

The philosopher Plato, who was Socrates's student, takes a step further to explain the essence and composition of the self. He had an interesting idea about the nature of the self. He believed that the self is primarily an intellectual entity and that its essence exists independently of the physical world.

In other words, according to Plato, who we truly are goes beyond our physical body and is rooted in our intellectual capabilities. This means that our true selves are not limited or defined by our physical surroundings but are instead connected to a deeper realm of knowledge and understanding (Valerio, 2019).

And finally, the Merriam-Webster Dictionary expounds on what the self consists of through its definition. According to Merriam-Webster, we're referring to the unique combination of different elements that make us who we are. These elements include things like our "body, emotions, thoughts, and sensations" (Merriam-Webster, 2023). It's the coming together of all these aspects that form the very essence of a person.

So, essentially, the union of these various elements shapes a person's individuality and identity.

What are the commonalities?

1. Self is not external; it is internal.
2. Self is not material; it is immaterial.
3. Self is not only your body but a combination of your soul and your body. Therefore, if you're hurting within and you're trying to feign happiness physically, you're hurting yourSELF.

What does this have to do with your happiness?

Socrates specifically explained that only when we truly know ourselves can we learn how to take care of ourselves. Without being aware of the "self," we'll always be in the dark about what we really need (Academy of Ideas, 2015). So, according to Socrates, getting to know ourselves is the first step toward living a fulfilling life.

You can't be truly compassionate toward yourself if you don't know who you are. So here it is, dear reader—the first step to being happy is: ***Know yourSELF, and you'll know what you need.***

- When you fail, what do you need?
- When you make a mistake, what do you need?
- When you couldn't meet a deadline, what do you need?

Self-compassion and happiness

When people around you are in need of love, a companion, comfort, or encouragement, you know what to do or say to make them feel better. You show compassion to them because you know what they need in that moment.

But when you find yourself in the same boat as those people, can you recognize what you need?

Recognizing your needs—physical, intellectual, and emotional—and serving yourSELF is being compassionate to yourSELF. That's the pathway to being happy.

But remember, to recognize your needs, you'll have to recline in your seat a bit and spend some time with yourself regularly to get to know yourself. You'll find out so many amazing things you didn't know about YOU before.

Try this short exercise:

- *Set aside about 20–30 minutes to be with yourself for the next seven days. During this time, ask yourself, "Who am I?" Document everything you discover in a journal.*

The Importance of Self-Compassion

Is self-compassion important? I can almost hear my inner being screaming, YES! After reading the previous section, you've probably deduced the importance of self-compassion.

Here are 15 benefits of self-compassion:

1. **Emotional wellbeing:** It nurtures positive emotions and reduces negative ones, leading to greater overall emotional wellbeing.
2. **Resilience:** It helps build resilience by providing a supportive and understanding inner voice during challenging times.
3. **Self-acceptance:** It fosters self-acceptance, allowing us to embrace our imperfections and recognize our inherent worthiness.
4. **Reduced self-criticism:** It decreases self-critical thoughts and reduces the tendency to be overly hard on oneself.

5. **Improved mental health:** It contributes to improved mental health outcomes, such as lower levels of anxiety and depression.
6. **Increased motivation:** It encourages self-motivation and the pursuit of personal growth and goals without harsh self-judgment.
7. **Healthier relationships:** By cultivating self-compassion, we develop healthier and more compassionate relationships with others.
8. **Stress reduction:** It helps to alleviate stress and promotes a greater sense of calm and relaxation.
9. **Enhanced self-care:** It encourages self-care practices, as we recognize the importance of attending to our own needs and wellbeing.
10. **Boosted self-confidence:** It boosts self-confidence and self-esteem, as we learn to treat ourselves with kindness and understanding.
11. **Improved decision-making:** It fosters a non-judgmental attitude, which supports clearer and more rational decision-making.
12. **Empathy for others:** By extending compassion to ourselves, we also develop greater empathy and compassion for others.

13. **Increased self-awareness:** Self-compassion cultivates self-awareness, allowing us to better understand our emotions, thoughts, and behaviors.
14. **Authentic self-expression:** It enables us to express ourselves authentically and embrace our true selves without fear of judgment.
15. **Happiness and life satisfaction:** Ultimately, self-compassion contributes to increased happiness and overall life satisfaction.

What Self-Compassion Is and Isn't

I've explained what self-compassion is, but just a little addition here. According to Dr. Emma Seppälä (2021), the Science Director of Stanford University's Center for Compassion and Altruism Research and Education, self-compassion means treating yourself with the same kindness and understanding that you would show to a friend who made a mistake or didn't meet expectations.

Instead of criticizing or berating your friend, you would likely offer a listening ear and remind them that mistakes are a normal part of life, right? Self-compassion is about extending that same gentle and supportive approach to yourself. It means acknowledging your own imperfections and being understanding, just as you would be with a friend.

Self-compassion is not...

- Self-pity

It is not about wallowing in self-pity or constantly seeking sympathy from others.

- Self-indulgence

It is not about indulging in unhealthy behaviors or making excuses for harmful actions.

- Selfishness

It does not promote selfishness or disregard the needs and feelings of others.

- Self-criticism

It is not about engaging in self-criticism or harsh self-judgment.

- Self-esteem

While related, self-compassion is not the same as self-esteem. It doesn't rely on external validation or comparisons to others.

- Self-denial

It is not about denying your own needs or sacrificing your wellbeing for the sake of others.

- Self-isolation

It does not encourage isolating oneself or avoiding social connections.

- Self-absorption

It is not about being self-absorbed or solely focused on one's own needs without considering others.

- Self-deception

It does not involve deceiving oneself or avoiding responsibility for one's actions.

- Self-judgment

It is not about judging oneself or engaging in a constant evaluation of one's personal worth based on achievements or failures.

- Self-comparison

It is not about constantly comparing oneself to others or striving for unrealistic standards.

- Self-doubt

It is not about harboring self-doubt or undermining one's own abilities and potential.

- Self-righteousness

It is not about adopting a self-righteous attitude or feeling superior to others.

- Self-ignorance

It is not about ignoring or neglecting self-awareness and personal growth.

There's this balanced outlook to self-compassion. It's just a nurturing way of relating to yourself and fostering kindness, understanding, and acceptance without falling into these misconceptions or extremes.

The Three Main Components

Dr. Kristin Neff, a psychologist and associate professor in the department of educational psychology at the University of Texas, did some groundbreaking research on self-compassion. In the course of her research, she came up with three components of self-compassion (Frank Porter Graham Program on Mindfulness & Self-Compassion, 2023). The three components of self-compassion are:

- Self-kindness
- Common humanity
- Mindfulness

Being self-compassionate is being kind to self

Being self-compassionate means treating ourselves with kindness instead of being overly critical when things go wrong. It's about understanding that it's normal to make mistakes and face difficulties in life. Rather than getting angry or ignoring pain, self-compassionate people show themselves gentleness and acceptance.

Being self-compassionate is accepting our humanity

When we're frustrated, it's easy to think we're the only ones going through tough times or making mistakes. But self-compassion reminds us that suffering and imperfection are part of being human. It's about recognizing that we're not alone in our struggles and that everyone experiences challenges and setbacks.

Being self-compassionate is being mindful of our situation

Self-compassion means finding a good balance when it comes to dealing with our negative emotions. It's about having a healthy approach and not letting them overwhelm us. It means neither suppressing nor exaggerating them. We achieve this by connecting our own experiences of suffering to the experiences of others, gaining a broader perspective. It also requires being mindful, which means observing our thoughts and feelings without judgment* or denial. Mindfulness helps us hold our pain with awareness, without getting overwhelmed by it or carried away by negative reactions.

*Do you want to become Your Own Best Friend? Check out the Worksheet #1 in the **BONUS** at the beginning of the book.

Understanding Self-Esteem

There's this folktale about a certain oak tree that I heard some years ago. The oak tree was majestic and stood tall in the midst of the forest. With its towering height and strong branches, the tree commanded admiration from all the surrounding trees. However, deep within, the tree had a secret struggle—it doubted its worth and felt insignificant compared to the other grand trees in the forest.

One day, a powerful storm swept through the forest. Fierce winds blew, rain poured, and thunder roared. The forest was in chaos. While other trees bowed, and some were uprooted, the oak tree stood tall, its roots firmly grounded. As the storm subsided, the oak realized something remarkable—it had weathered the tempest with resilience and strength.

Word of its unwavering presence during the storm spread throughout the forest. Other trees, once envious of the oak's stature, began seeking its guidance and protection. The oak humbly shared its knowledge, offering shelter and support to those in need.

This made the oak realize the significance of its unwavering presence. It understood that its unique qualities and strength were valuable contributions to the forest ecosystem.

What does this mean for our discussion of self-esteem? Well, sometimes you don't know how much you're worth until your strength is put to the test.

What is self-esteem?

Cherry (2022) describes self-esteem as how you see yourself and how much you value yourself. It's like having a personal measure of how much you respect and believe in your own abilities and qualities. In a nutshell, it's about how confident you feel about yourself.

Your self-esteem has an impact on various aspects of your life. It can influence:

- How much you like and appreciate yourself as an individual
- Your ability to make decisions and confidently express your thoughts and opinions
- Your recognition of your own strengths and abilities
- Your willingness to step out of your comfort zone and tackle new or challenging tasks
- The level of kindness and compassion you show yourself
- How you handle mistakes without unfairly blaming and criticizing yourself
- Your ability to prioritize and take time for self-care and personal wellbeing
- Your belief that you are important and worthy, just as you are
- Your belief that you deserve happiness and fulfillment in life

According to Trzesniewski et al. (2003), self-esteem usually starts off lower in childhood and then tends to grow as we become teenagers and adults. Eventually, it reaches a point where it becomes relatively steady and consistent. It's kind of like how our personality traits also tend to stay fairly stable over time. So, just like our personalities, our self-esteem develops and solidifies as we grow older.

When You Have Low Self-Esteem

As a teen, I used to struggle to air my opinions in class. Even when I knew the answer to a question, at best, it stayed in my head and I kept quiet because I was always afraid of what others would think if I got it wrong.

I was in a chemistry class one day and our chemistry teacher asked a question. Not even the brightest students in the class could answer it, but I knew the answer. The answer kept dancing somewhere in my head but couldn't step out of my mouth. I doubted myself. If the best students in the class couldn't answer the question, who was I to do so?

The teacher had a mix of disappointment and frustration written on her face. After waiting for someone to answer her question (no one did), she answered it herself. Fortunately for me, I was correct, but only in my head. The guilt of not being bold enough to say the answer that day lingered with me for a while. Later on, I criticized myself for not being brave enough to answer.

I'm a better adult now. But the scars from not believing in myself while growing up remain.

—*Lucas*

Low self-esteem is like having a little voice in your head that constantly puts you down. It tells you things like "You're no good," "You're overweight," "What's the point?", or "You're not capable of doing this." It's that negative chatter that undermines your confidence and makes you doubt yourself.

What happens when you have low self-esteem?

- Persistent self-doubt
- Feelings of worthlessness or inadequacy
- Fear of judgment or rejection by others
- Difficulty in asserting oneself or setting boundaries
- Always needing validation and approval from others
- Avoidance of new challenges or opportunities due to fear of failure
- Negative self-talk and self-criticism
- Lack of self-confidence and self-belief
- Tendency to compare oneself unfavorably to others
- Vulnerability to anxiety, depression, or other mental health issues
- Difficulty in maintaining healthy relationships
- Reduced motivation and ambition

- Social withdrawal or isolation
- Increased susceptibility to peer pressure or manipulation
- Limited belief in one's own abilities and potential

What causes low self-esteem?

From my personal experience and reflection, I know that low self-esteem can be caused by one or more of the following:

- Bullying or experiencing abuse
- Prejudice, discrimination, or stigma (e.g., racism)
- Job loss or difficulty finding employment
- Work or study-related challenges
- Physical health issues
- Mental health challenges
- Relationship difficulties, separation, or divorce
- Financial or housing problems
- Concerns about appearance and body image
- Feeling pressured to meet unrealistic expectations (e.g., from social media)
- Childhood experiences of neglect or emotional/physical abuse
- Critical or unsupportive parenting
- Academic or athletic failures

- Chronic stress or trauma
- Unhealthy or toxic relationships
- Social isolation or loneliness
- Feeling like a failure in achieving personal goals
- Cultural or societal pressure to conform
- Internalizing negative messages from media or society
- Perfectionism and fear of making mistakes
- Unresolved past traumas or emotional wounds
- Chronic illness or disability
- Feelings of unworthiness due to past mistakes or regrets

You may have gone through some of these things, or you might have faced challenges that aren't mentioned here. It's also possible that there isn't just one specific cause for your low self-esteem.

If you're dealing with low self-esteem, making a change might seem hard. But don't worry, there are things you can do to improve it. There's hope for you.

Here are some simple actions you can take:

- **Be mindful of negative thoughts.** Pay attention to those sneaky negative thoughts that affect how you see yourself. Recognize them and challenge their accuracy.

- **Question negative thinking patterns.** When negative thoughts arise, challenge them by replacing them with more realistic and positive ones.
- **Embrace positive self-talk.** Repeat positive affirmations to yourself, like a mini pep talk that uplifts your spirits (Cascio et al., 2015).
- **Cultivate self-compassion.** Practice forgiveness for past mistakes and accept yourself as a whole, including your flaws and imperfections. Move forward with kindness and understanding.

The Role of Self-Compassion in Self-Esteem and Overall Wellbeing

Self-compassion plays a crucial role in shaping one's self-esteem. By cultivating self-compassion, you can develop a healthier and more positive relationship with yourself, which in turn positively impacts your self-esteem and overall sense of wellbeing. Self-compassion involves treating yourself with kindness, understanding, and acceptance, particularly in times of difficulty or self-judgment. It means acknowledging that everyone makes mistakes and experiences challenges, and extending the same compassion and support to yourself as you would to a close friend or loved one.

Practicing self-compassion has been shown to have a multitude of benefits. Here are some key points to consider:

1. **Enhances self-esteem:** Self-compassion helps individuals develop a kind and nurturing inner voice, counteracting the negative self-talk that often accompanies low self-esteem. By treating oneself with compassion, individuals can foster a greater sense of self-worth and appreciation.
2. **Reduces self-criticism:** Engaging in self-compassion practices helps individuals let go of harsh self-judgment and self-criticism. It encourages self-acceptance and self-forgiveness, leading to a more positive and nurturing mindset.
3. **Cultivates emotional resilience:** Self-compassion allows individuals to acknowledge and validate their emotions without judgment. By practicing self-compassion, individuals build emotional resilience, allowing them to navigate life's challenges with greater ease and bounce back from setbacks.
4. **Supports overall wellbeing:** Self-compassion contributes to a sense of overall wellbeing by promoting self-care, stress reduction, and positive self-regard. It encourages individuals to prioritize their physical, mental, and emotional needs, leading to improved overall health and happiness.

Common Self-Compassion Misconceptions

Earlier in this chapter, I told you what self-compassion isn't. As I close this chapter, I want to emphasize again some misconceptions you might have about self-compassion—and these come from the pioneer of the concept itself, Dr. Kristin Neff.

Dr. Neff (2020) shares the five top myths about self-compassion:

- Myth 1: Self-compassion is equivalent to self-pity.
- Myth 2: Self-compassion is a sign of weakness.
- Myth 3: Self-compassion leads to complacency.
- Myth 4: Self-compassion is narcissistic.
- Myth 5: Self-compassion is selfish.

In reality, it's not any of those. Dr. Neff concludes by stating that self-compassion taps into our ability to love, be wise, show courage, and be generous. It's a state of mind and heart that knows no boundaries and doesn't require a specific path. It's accessible to every individual just by being human.

Chapter Takeaway

This chapter has given us a solid foundation for the whole essence of this book. If you've skipped any section in this chapter, you've missed a foundational building block in this book, so please make sure you've read through the entire chapter.

Our starting point in this book stressed the importance of understanding the self. Since the core message of this book is directed towards just one person, YOU, it's essential to have an understanding of yourself before you can direct any form of care towards yourself. An understanding of yourself will help you know what you need and how to cater to those needs.

Also, don't forget that the value you place on yourself has an effect on your wellbeing. Prioritize self-compassion and cultivate self-esteem, and you'll be signing yourself up for happiness.

CHAPTER 2

The Psychology of Happiness

"To the person who pleases him, God gives wisdom, knowledge and happiness."

—Ecclesiastes 2:26

"One of the secrets of a happy life is continuous small treats."

—Iris Murdoch

Emily, a typical millennial young woman who had always believed that external achievements and material possessions were the keys to happiness, worked tirelessly to climb the corporate ladder. She accumulated a lavish lifestyle and chased after societal ideals of success.

Despite her accomplishments, Emily felt a lingering sense of emptiness and dissatisfaction. She constantly yearned for more, believing that the next promotion, bigger house, or luxury purchase would finally bring her the happiness she sought.

Unfortunately, that vacuum kept expanding with each new accomplishment. She kept craving more. Frustrated, Emily began to wonder why, despite all she had acquired, that vacuum within her hadn't been filled yet.

She asked questions. She kept looking for answers. Finally, she found one in the most unlikely of places. She stumbled upon an old classmate from college at a mall and the two of them stopped to catch up. Emily discovered something that day: her old classmate wasn't living an exotic life like she was, yet she was happy and felt fulfilled. Emily had been looking for happiness in all the wrong places all this time.

I dare say that everyone longs to be happy, but obviously, not everyone *is* genuinely happy. As I delve into this discussion on happiness, please indulge me for a moment and respond to this question:

What can give you (not us) the happiness you long for? Have you found it yet?

Happiness: A Mood or a Feeling?

What do you associate with happiness?

Christmas is a special time of the year that many people look forward to. Oh, how they love the Yuletide season and that giddy sensation that grows larger in their hearts as Christmas approaches. Having loved ones around and being able to share the love and joy of the season with other people is usually the high point of the holiday.

Would you call that sensation during the Christmas season a feeling of happiness or a mood of happiness?

Well, you wouldn't be wrong if you called it a mood or a feeling. But whether you call it a mood or a feeling, I'd like you to bear in mind that both of these descriptions are temporal and imply that happiness is subject to external factors, like events, occasions, and seasons.

Is happiness a mood?

Foster (2013) states that researchers in anthropology and psychology have identified six primary emotions commonly experienced by humans: joy, distress, anger, fear, surprise, and disgust. Foster adds that some people also include happiness and sadness in this list, while others consider these to be moods rather than emotions.

However, Foster's stance on happiness is that when it comes to defining happiness as either an emotion or a mood, she personally finds it more sensible to consider it a mood. For instance, when she's in a happy mood, she tends to experience the emotion of joy more frequently, and it takes a lot to bring about the emotion of distress.

Is happiness a feeling?

Cherry (2022), in contrast, calls happiness a feeling—usually, happiness is when we feel joyful, satisfied, content, and fulfilled. She agrees, however, that although happiness can have various meanings, it's often described as having positive emotions and feeling satisfied with life.

Ackerman (2019) adds that happiness is often associated with experiencing pleasure and contentment. It's important to note that happiness is different from intense feelings like joy, ecstasy, or bliss.

Another school of thought says that happiness is ***a state of mind***. Kashyap (2022) writes in the *Hindustan Times* that happiness is all about feeling good and having a positive mindset. It's something we can work on and develop within ourselves. The best part is that we get to choose whether we want to be happy or not. It's like having a remote control for our emotions! We have the power to decide how we feel. Remember, what we focus on tends to shape our experiences, so it's important to direct our attention towards the things that bring us joy and positivity.

My take

Whether you believe that happiness is a mood, a feeling, a state of mind, or a choice you're poised to make daily, I'd say whichever you go for, ensure you don't settle for anything transient.

If you think it's a mood or a feeling, you'll be inclined to believe that your happiness is tied to certain events, people, circumstances, or occasions. You don't expect those external factors to always happen, do you? And you don't expect them to always produce the same emotional energy, do you?

So think it through before you stick with an opinion. Stick with a definition that's not subject to time and seasons.

What Is True Happiness?

Purohit (2022) states that no one in this world has the exact answer to what true happiness really means because true happiness can mean different things to different people; we all have unique definitions and experiences of what makes us truly happy. And I think he's right.

Some people have emphatically proclaimed that happiness doesn't rely on what's happening around us or the circumstances we find ourselves in. It's not just a state of mind, either, but rather an attitude that comes from deep within the heart. It's about how we choose to approach life and the perspective we adopt.

So, ***happiness is an attitude that flows from deep within***. I do concur!

In line with this thought, Julia Roberts, who starred as Elizabeth Robert in the biographical drama *Eat, Pray, Love*, says that happiness is something that doesn't just fall into our laps. It's the result of our personal efforts. We have to fight for it, work hard for it, and never give up on it.

Sometimes, we may even go on adventures and explore the world in search of it. We need to actively engage in the things that bring us joy and appreciate the blessings that come our way. Once we've found happiness, we can't become complacent. It's essential to continuously strive to maintain happiness. We must keep putting in the effort to stay afloat and keep swimming towards happiness.

This also means that ***true happiness is an attitude that must be cultivated and nurtured over time.***

To achieve this, here are a few practical tips for you:

- **Be your own best friend:** Treat yourself with love and kindness, just like you would treat a prince or princess.
- **Surround yourself with positivity:** Stay away from people who bring negativity into your life.
- **Let go of negative emotions:** Avoid feelings of envy, jealousy, fear, and anger as much as possible.
- **Take care of your wellbeing:** Nourish your body and soul by eating nutritious meals and practicing meditation.
- **Enjoy your own company:** Set aside time for yourself to engage in activities like reading, writing, or watching a movie at home. Embrace the opportunity to be alone without fearing it.

- **Make a pact with yourself:** Commit to treating yourself in the best possible way, with love, respect, and self-care.
- **Practice kindness and humility:** Start by being kind and humble towards yourself, and then extend that same kindness and humility to others.
- **Engage in small acts of selflessness:** Spread positivity by smiling at strangers or offering your seat to someone in need on public transport.

Remember, happiness starts from within, and by taking these small steps, you can create a more joyful and fulfilling life.

The Role Our Brain Plays

Our brain plays a significant role in shaping our happiness and wellbeing (Hanson, 2013; Nesse, 2000). As human beings, we have inherited a complex brain that has evolved over millions of years and has shaped our thoughts, emotions, and behaviors in various ways.

One key aspect of our brain's role in happiness is its ability to regulate our emotions (Siegel, 2007). The limbic system, which includes structures like the amygdala and hippocampus, is responsible for processing emotions and forming memories. These brain regions help us experience and process both positive and negative emotions, which ultimately impact our overall happiness.

Furthermore, our brain is wired for social connection and belonging (Hanson, 2013). The prefrontal cortex, a part of the brain involved in social cognition and decision-making, allows us to form and maintain relationships, empathize with others, and experience feelings of love and belonging. These social connections and a sense of belonging are crucial for our happiness and wellbeing.

The brain is also equipped with a phenomenon called the "negativity bias" (Hanson, 2013). This means it has a tendency to pay more attention to negative experiences or threats in order to ensure our survival. While this bias helped our ancestors avoid danger, in today's world, it can lead to a greater focus on negativity and a reduced emphasis on positive experiences. Understanding this bias can help us consciously shift our attention toward positive aspects of life, cultivating happiness in the process.

It's important to note that our brain's influence on happiness is not fixed or predetermined. Through neuroplasticity, our brain has the remarkable ability to adapt and change throughout our lives (Davidson & Begley, 2012). We can actively engage in practices like mindfulness, positive affirmations, gratitude, and acts of kindness, which can reshape the neural pathways in our brain, fostering greater happiness and wellbeing.*

*Explore the Self-Care Wheel and practice your Perfect Self-Care Day. Look for Worksheet 7 when you download the **BONUS**.

"Uhhh, Sir, I don't want to interrupt your meditation but we're live on air."

Why We Feel the Way We Do: The Psychology of Moods

Have you ever wondered why you feel the way you do in a given situation? Our moods are complex and can be influenced by various psychological factors. Let's take a closer look at the psychology of moods and why they occur.

1. Moods are often described as prolonged emotional states that can last for hours or even days. They are different from emotions, which are shorter-lived and more specific in nature. Moods tend to be less intense and have a broader range of emotional experiences.

2. One of the factors that influence our moods is our thoughts and beliefs. Our interpretation of events and situations can shape how we feel. For example, if we perceive a situation as threatening, we may experience anxiety or fear. On the other hand, if we view a situation positively, we may feel happiness or excitement.

3. Our behaviors and actions also play a role in our moods. Engaging in activities that we enjoy or that align with our values can boost our mood. Similarly, negative behaviors or situations can contribute to negative moods. For instance, if we constantly engage in self-critical thoughts or surround ourselves with negative influences, it can lead to feelings of sadness or frustration.

4. Social factors are another important aspect of our moods. Our interactions with others, such as receiving social support or facing social rejection, can impact how

we feel. Positive social connections and a sense of belonging can enhance our mood, while loneliness or conflicts can lead to negative emotions.

5. Biological factors, including our brain chemistry and hormones, also play a role in our moods. Neurotransmitters like serotonin and dopamine influence our emotional wellbeing. Additionally, hormonal changes, such as those during menstruation or menopause, can affect mood stability.
6. Environmental factors, such as our physical surroundings and the weather, can influence our moods as well. For example, being in a pleasant environment or experiencing sunny weather can boost our mood, while a gloomy or stressful environment can contribute to negative feelings.
7. It's important to remember that our moods can fluctuate throughout the day and are influenced by a combination of these factors. Understanding the psychology of moods can help us become more aware of our emotional experiences and develop strategies to manage and improve our overall wellbeing.

Factors That Influence Your Mood

I'm sure you've experienced having your mood take a sudden dip and become negative. There are several factors at play that contribute to why this can happen, including biological, psychological, and environmental influences (Monitoring-your-mood, n.d.).

Let's take a closer look at some common factors that affect our moods.

- Stress

We all know that stress can weigh us down and put us in a sour mood. Whether it's work deadlines, relationship issues, or financial pressures, stress has a way of casting a shadow over our emotions.

- Poor sleep, fatigue, and overwork

When we're running on empty, lacking sleep and feeling exhausted, it's no wonder our mood takes a hit. Burning the candle at both ends can leave us feeling irritable and cranky.

- Hangry moments

Ever experienced that sudden shift in mood when you're desperately in need of food? When your stomach starts rumbling, your mood can quickly plummet. It's amazing how a satisfying meal can turn things around.

- Social interactions

Our encounters with other people can have a surprising impact on our mood. A rude comment, a friendly gesture, or an awkward encounter can all contribute to how we feel in the moment.

- The news

Oh, the power of the media! Sometimes, getting bombarded with negative news stories can leave us feeling down and disheartened. It's hard to stay upbeat when the headlines are constantly filled with doom and gloom.

- The weather

Nature has a way of influencing our mood. Rainy days can make us feel a bit gloomy, while sunny weather can lift our spirits. It's like our mood takes a cue from the sky.

- Hormonal rollercoaster

We can't forget about the influence of hormones on our mood. From the ups and downs of puberty to the hormonal shifts that occur during a woman's menstrual cycle, pregnancy, and menopause, our mood can go for a wild ride.

- Lack of exercise

When we've been sitting around like couch potatoes for too long, our mood can suffer. Getting our bodies moving and engaging in physical activity can do wonders for our mental wellbeing.

- Lack of break time

Sometimes, we're just in dire need of a break, whether it's from the daily grind at work or responsibilities at home. Taking some time off and rejuvenating can work wonders for our mood.

And let's not forget these factors as well:

- Colors

Believe it or not, certain colors can affect our mood. Bright and vibrant colors can uplift us, while dull and muted tones may have a more negative impact.

- Dehydration

Our body's cry for water can also impact our mood. When we're not drinking enough water, it can leave us feeling sluggish and irritable.

- Social media

Ah, the double-edged sword of social media. While it can connect us with others, it can also contribute to negative emotions. Comparing ourselves to others' highlight reels or getting caught up in online drama can definitely put a damper on our mood.

- Posture

Yes, even our posture can influence how we feel. Slouching and hunching can make us feel down, while standing tall and confidently can give us a mood boost.

- Partner's mood

The vibes from our significant other can have a ripple effect on our own mood. When our partner is in a grumpy mood, it can be contagious and bring us down too.

- Physical space

The environment we're in can impact our mood. Cluttered spaces or a lack of organization can create a sense of chaos and negatively affect our emotions.

- Temperature

Believe it or not, the temperature around us can play a role in our mood. Being too hot or too cold can leave us feeling uncomfortable and affect our overall wellbeing.

- Menstrual cycle

Ladies may experience mood swings or changes in emotional wellbeing as a result of their monthly cycle.

- Diet

What we eat can have an influence on our mood. A poor diet lacking in essential nutrients can leave us feeling sluggish and less than cheerful.

So, the next time you find yourself in a funk, remember that there could be a whole range of factors at play. From stress and sleep to the weather and even colors, the world around us has a funny way of shaping our mood.

The Link Between Your Feelings and Actions

The relationship between our feelings and actions is a complex and intertwined one. Have you ever responded poorly to a simple question such as, "Excuse me, where's the restroom?" because you were angry?

Did you know you could have responded to certain inquiries differently if you were feeling differently?

Obviously, our emotions can significantly influence the way we behave and the choices we make. Here are some key points to consider:

Positive emotions, such as joy, contentment, and love, have a tendency to drive pro-social behaviors and acts of kindness. When we feel happy and fulfilled, we are more likely to extend that positivity to others.

Negative emotions, like anger, sadness, or fear, can sometimes lead to impulsive or aggressive behaviors if not effectively managed. It is crucial to recognize and regulate these emotions to avoid any harmful actions.

Our feelings of motivation and enthusiasm can serve as powerful catalysts for action, propelling us toward our goals and prompting us to engage in activities that bring us fulfillment. When we feel inspired and driven, we are more likely to take steps towards personal growth and achievement.

Emotions like guilt or remorse can act as signals for us to reflect on our actions and behaviors. They prompt us to take responsibility, apologize, make amends, or change our behavior to rectify a situation. These emotions can serve as a catalyst for personal growth and learning.

Finally, it is important to note that the relationship between feelings and actions is not one-sided. While emotions can influence our behaviors, our actions can also impact our emotions. Engaging in positive actions can generate positive emotions, creating a positive feedback loop.

Common Happiness Misconceptions

Humans are naturally inclined to think negatively. I believe that our negativity contributes to a lot of the misconceptions prevalent in our society.

There are many misconceptions surrounding the concept of happiness. People often have preconceived notions about what it takes to be happy and what happiness truly means. Here are some of those misconceptions about happiness:

- The more money you have, the happier you'll be.
- True happiness is found in the act of giving alone, not in receiving.
- Having too much freedom of choice can reduce happiness.
- Happiness is the only way to find joy.
- Happiness is a destination.
- Happiness conflicts with a mature sense of purpose.
- Happiness is all about selfishness.
- No one can recreate happiness.
- The best times are over for us.
- Happiness is solely about goals.

- Longer vacations aren't always worth it.
- No one should try to be happy all the time.

Misconceptions such as these are sometimes the product of fear and ignorance. The only way to debunk them is to know the truth! The truth sets us free.

Will I Ever Find Happiness?

I won't dive into a long discussion about this—the outright answer is a resounding YES!

Remember, you can't find happiness in anything external. You'll have to look within. That's the attitude you need to cultivate and nurture daily.

You deserve to be happy.

Chapter Takeaway

I hope this chapter has been truly enlightening for you in redefining concepts, debunking myths, and realigning you to the true meaning of things.

In this chapter, we've explained that happiness is not transient. It's something we can experience every day as an attitude. But it needs to be cultivated and nurtured. We're not inherently wired to live that way, but we can reprogram ourselves to live a happy life every day.

Don't rely on feelings and moods to determine your happiness because they're subject to external factors themselves. If you feel you really need to settle on a particular definition of happiness, at least don't settle for anything transient.

PART 2

Improving Emotional Health

I invite you to explore with me the incredible power of mindful self-compassion. It's one of the super keys to having stable emotional health.

Are you wondering how treating yourself with kindness and understanding can lead to greater happiness? Well, that's one of the things you're about to discover in this part of the book.

Although we had a discussion on self-esteem and its impact on your wellbeing in the previous part, we'll expound on it more deeply in Chapter 4 and discover how it is connected to your happiness. Just so you know, strong positive self-esteem paves the way for a happier and more confident existence. You don't want to miss out on these strategies for building your self-esteem.

Throughout the fifth chapter, we will explore practical ways to boost emotional health and enhance our mood. You'll learn the intricacies of emotional regulation and how to apply it to enhance your emotional wellbeing.

The final chapter in this part addresses a sensitive issue: depression. Depression is a bane in our society today, and I can tell you that it's so real. Dealing with depression can be incredibly challenging, but it is important to remember that there is hope and support available. There are diverse techniques outlined in this chapter that you can apply. You could also recommend them to someone that you know has been having a difficult time in their life.

I would describe this part of the book as a redemptive and curative section where you'll receive instructions that will guide you to receive healing and restoration for your soul. By delving into these topics, you will be equipped with valuable knowledge and practical tools to navigate life's challenges and cultivate a profound sense of happiness and wellbeing.

The wisdom in this part is bubbling forth; let's sit and drink together, shall we?

CHAPTER 3

Mindful Self-Compassion

"I rejoice in following your statutes as one rejoices in great riches. I meditate on your precepts and consider your ways. I delight in your decrees;I will not neglect your word."

—Psalms 119: 14-16

"Healing takes self-compassion."

—Juansen Dizon

Recently, I a new friend of mine unexpectedly canceled our meetup for the third time. I felt a wave of hurt, sadness, and disappointment wash over me. It wasn't easy, but I knew this was an opportunity to practice mindfulness and emotional healing.

So, I settled down in a comfortable place and took a moment to check in with myself. Instead of seeking distractions, I chose to sit with these emotions and explore their underlying messages.

As I turned my attention inward, I noticed the extent of the hurt within. I felt scared, abandoned, neglected, and rejected. I couldn't discard those feelings—they were valid. And I couldn't suppress them because to do that would be to aggravate the hurt. I didn't take it out on my new friend either; rather, I chose to look within and offered myself compassion and support.

My new friend was going through her own struggles. Allowing her situation to keep influencing my emotions would only expose me to more pain. So, I stopped getting my hopes up when it came to her. This affected our relationship, but it was worth it. I needed to heal from the series of emotional wounds first. And I had to protect my mind as well.

Through this experience, I grew as a person and learned to take better care of my inner self. I'm still on a journey of learning and growth, knowing that when things become painful, mindfulness and self-compassion are more essential than ever.

Mindfulness in the Self-Compassion Context

Mindfulness and self-compassion are the latest trends in self-improvement. But here's what's more fascinating about them: there's actually a number of ongoing studies all around the world that are exploring how these practices can seriously improve your mental health (Turow, 2023).

So far, the results of that research have made it pretty clear that mindfulness and self-compassion really do work and have some amazing benefits. It's pretty awesome to see how and why these practices make such a positive impact, don't you think?

My emphasis, however, is not on how these practices work together to enhance your wellbeing, but on how one of the practices enhances the other. What role does mindfulness play in making self-compassion more effective? That's the question in this section.

We should start with an understanding of mindfulness. ***What is mindfulness?***

Scott (2022a) defines mindfulness as being fully aware of the present moment without any judgments or distractions from the past or future. It involves tuning in to your senses and paying attention to things like your breath or the sensations in your body. The main idea is to be fully "in the now" and not let your mind wander.

Crumpler (2022) adds that mindfulness is all about consciously and gently directing one's attention to the present moment—essentially, reminding yourself to stay focused on what's happening right now. By contrast, having a mind full of divergent thoughts means you're not fully rooted in the present moment.

How can I be mindfully self-compassionate?

Through mindfulness, you can quickly identify negative, critical thoughts about yourself when they arise. This quick identification will help you to:

- Gather your thoughts and focus on the issue at hand, not the past or what is yet to happen.
- Respond to your thoughts and feelings in a non-judgmental way.
- Respond with kindness and compassion to release negative thoughts and emotions before they escalate and have a negative effect on you.

"I'd be more convinced we weren't lost if the map wasn't upside-down."

Overcoming Barriers to Self-Compassion

Did you know that being kind to yourself can have some amazing benefits for your health? It turns out that self-compassion is linked to things like having better relationships, improved physical health, and the ability to bounce back during tough times (MacBeth & Gumley, 2012). Even though lots of research has shown how great it is for our wellbeing, many people still find it hard to actually practice self-compassion (Gilbert et al., 2011).

Here are a few reasons some people find it hard to practice self-compassion.

1. **Feeling "not good enough" and being too hard on ourselves:** Sometimes we get caught up in negative thoughts and criticize ourselves too much. We may strive for perfection and constantly feel unworthy, which makes it difficult to show ourselves compassion.
2. **Struggling with overwhelming emotions:** When we're dealing with intense emotions like sadness, anger, or fear, it can be hard to offer ourselves kindness. We may get stuck in the grip of these emotions and forget to be gentle and understanding toward ourselves.
3. **Feeling like self-compassion is pointless:** Some people might question the purpose of self-compassion. They may think it's selfish or unnecessary to focus on caring for themselves when there are so many other things to worry about. This mindset can prevent them from practicing self-compassion.
4. **Difficulty with the concept of "self-compassion":** The term "self-compassion" itself can be confusing or off-putting to some individuals. They might associate it with self-indulgence or view it as a sign of weakness.

This misunderstanding can create a barrier to actually embracing self-compassion.

5. **Being trapped in a cycle of harsh self-judgment:** Many of us have a habit of being overly critical and harsh towards ourselves. This inner voice of self-judgment can be relentless, making it hard to show ourselves the kindness and understanding we truly deserve.
6. **Believing self-compassion is too touchy-feely or weak:** Some people perceive self-compassion as something overly sentimental or soft. They may think it goes against being strong and resilient. This misconception can make them hesitant to practice self-compassion.
7. **Feeling overwhelmed by the idea of self-compassion:** For some individuals, the idea of showing themselves compassion can feel overwhelming. They may not know where to start or how to integrate it into their lives. This overwhelm can hinder them from embracing self-compassion.
8. **Lack of experience receiving compassion from others:** If someone has had limited or no experience receiving compassion and understanding from others, they may find it difficult to extend the same kindness

to themselves. They may not have a reference point for what self-compassion looks or feels like.

How can you overcome these barriers to self-compassion?

1. **Recognize your worth and challenge self-criticism:** Remind yourself that you are deserving of kindness and understanding, just like anyone else. When self-critical thoughts arise, question their validity and replace them with more compassionate and realistic self-talk.
2. **Embrace and validate your emotions:** Instead of pushing away or suppressing your emotions, allow yourself to feel them without judgment. Practice self-compassion by acknowledging your emotions, offering yourself comfort, and seeking healthy ways to cope with them.
3. **Find meaning in self-compassion:** Understand that self-compassion is not selfish but rather a vital component of overall wellbeing. Recognize that taking care of yourself allows you to be more present and available to help others in a meaningful way.
4. **Reframe the concept:** If the term "self-compassion" feels off-putting, reframe it in a way that resonates with you. Think of it as self-care, self-kindness, or simply treating yourself with the same understanding and support you would offer a friend.

5. **Challenge the inner critic:** Whenever your inner voice becomes harsh or judgmental, consciously choose to counteract it with self-kindness. Treat yourself with the same compassion and encouragement you would extend to a loved one facing similar challenges.
6. **Understand the strength in self-compassion:** Recognize that self-compassion is not a sign of weakness but rather a display of inner strength and resilience. It takes courage to acknowledge your vulnerabilities and offer yourself the care and support you need.
7. **Take small steps and be patient:** Overcoming barriers to self-compassion can be a gradual process. Start with small acts of self-kindness and build from there. Remember, it's okay to take it one step at a time and be patient with yourself along the way.
8. **Seek out compassionate support:** Surround yourself with individuals who demonstrate compassion and understanding. Engage in conversations or seek guidance from supportive friends, family, or professionals who can help you navigate and cultivate self-compassion.

How to Practice Self-Compassion

Self-compassion is all about being kind to ourselves, even when things feel tough. It's not just about feeling good; it's about showing ourselves goodwill. When we practice self-compassion, we acknowledge that the present moment may be painful, but we choose to be mindful and respond with kindness and care. We also remind ourselves that it's okay to be imperfect because that's something all human beings experience (Neff, 2019).

Here are a number of ways I believe you can practice self-compassion:

Treat yourself like a friend

Start by imagining how you would treat someone you care about. We can't always take away their pain, but we can acknowledge it and offer support to help them through it. So, let's apply the same kindness to ourselves. It's okay to make mistakes and be human. Just like you wouldn't judge a friend for being lazy or missing a call, give yourself the same understanding and cut yourself some slack. Remember, imperfection is part of being human, and you're not alone in that.

Take care of yourself as you would others

This tip goes hand in hand with the previous one. Just like you would comfort a friend in need, show the same care and empathy towards yourself. When a friend is feeling down, you might give them a pat on the back or hold their hand to provide comfort. Well, guess what? You can do those things for yourself too! It may feel a bit strange at first, but try using tender and forgiving language with yourself, like calling yourself "darling" or "sweetheart."

These small gestures can activate your caregiving system and release oxytocin, which has positive effects on your heart. Don't worry if it feels a bit awkward; you can adjust the endearing terms to something that feels more natural to you. The key is to treat yourself with kindness and understanding.

Quiet your inner critic

Did you know that you are most likely your own toughest critic? Have you ever had those negative thoughts like, "I dressed nicely today, but I still don't look as good as those guys in GQ magazine" or "I got a pay raise, but it's just not enough"? We often fall into the trap of constantly wanting more and comparing ourselves to others, which leads to negative thinking.

Negativity is the enemy of self-compassion. It's easy to be negative, but it's not helpful. We're often kind and supportive to our close friends, yet we can be so hard on ourselves, creating a downward spiral of self-criticism.

So, how do you break free from this negative thought loop?

Silence that self-critical voice.

Boost your emotional awareness

A great way to cultivate self-compassion is learning to identify and label your emotions. By doing this, you can understand what they're trying to tell you about the things that truly matter in your life.

Try journaling

Writing in a journal can be a helpful practice in developing a better understanding of your inner experiences. It gives you a chance to expand your vocabulary and gain insights into your emotions.

Recognize feelings and needs in others

As you become more comfortable with acknowledging your own feelings and needs, you'll start noticing them in the people around you too. Whether it's your manager, colleagues, partner, or family members, developing this awareness of their emotions is an important part of self-compassion.

Remember that shared humanity matters

Connecting with others and recognizing our shared humanity is crucial for cultivating self-compassion. When we understand that others have similar desires and struggles, it becomes easier to extend compassion and empathy toward them.

Try "releasing statements"

Positive affirmations may not resonate with everyone, and that's okay. If you find them unnatural or ineffective, you can try something called "releasing statements." These statements are like exercises in self-forgiveness and detached non-judgment. When you catch yourself thinking a negative thought, like, "I'm such a horrible person for getting upset," try flipping it around and "releasing" yourself from that feeling. For example, say to yourself, "It's okay that I felt upset."

Embrace self-acceptance

Self-acceptance means embracing both your perceived shortcomings and your character strengths. Self-compassion involves not blowing up these shortcomings to define who you are. Instead, remember that thoughts and feelings are simply behaviors and states.

Practice mindfulness

Mindfulness practices are a great way to stay present in the moment. They are not only core components of self-compassion but can also be done anytime and anywhere. Activities like deep breathing, body scans, and the "self-compassion break" can help you cultivate mindfulness.

Avoid quick judgments

Don't assume that you will always behave a certain way. For example, instead of thinking, "I always get grumpy and antisocial on flights," give yourself the benefit of the doubt. Treat yourself* as you would treat others, and be open to the possibility of acting differently in different situations.

*Do you want to host a "Compliment Shower" for yourself? **Check out** the exercises of Worksheet #3 when you download the **BONUS.**

The Role of Self-Acceptance

To be kind to ourselves, we must learn to accept who we are—but it's easy to get confused about what it really means to "accept" oneself. When someone tells us to accept something, we might think they're telling us to just tolerate it or deal with it.

But acceptance is actually a much stronger and more helpful tool than that. It doesn't mean giving up or surrendering. Acceptance is about recognizing where we are right now, which is crucial in figuring out how to move forward from that point (Hannan, 2020).

Sakhaee (2019) notes that acceptance ought to be accompanied by a genuine willingness to evolve, contribute, and focus on one's values, strengths, and interests. The truth is that when we accept ourselves as we are, we shift from being our own adversary to our own ally. Carl Rogers (cited by Sakhaee, 2019), a key figure in humanistic psychology, observed that true self-acceptance leads to personal change. It is a transformative process.

What's really interesting is that the initial step towards change isn't about judging ourselves—it's about accepting who we are. That's the crucial part, even though it might go against what we usually think. Embracing our imperfections actually helps us be more genuine and authentic. When we practice acceptance, we don't feel the need to defend or deny our flaws, which tends to happen when we're not accepting. This opens the door to more effective change as we examine our flaws with acceptance, compassion, and curiosity.

It all begins with a simple act of self-love, even in moments when you're angry, scared, confused, or tired (Fahkry, 2017).

I'll give you a few indicators that you're not accepting yourself as you ought to:

- Always feeling discouraged
- Dealing with depression
- Experiencing anxiety
- Experiencing fear, particularly social fears
- Avoiding people and situations that may trigger negative emotions
- Struggling with self-loathing
- Overachieving or underachieving

- Having difficulties with setting healthy relationship boundaries and experiencing relationship problems
- Engaging in negative self-talk

You wouldn't be experiencing all of these if you took the bold step to embrace yourself and work on yourself to become better.

4 ways to practice self-acceptance

- Practice self-compassion:
    - Be kind to yourself
    - Be mindful of your feelings
    - Permit yourself to have flaws
- Be non-judgmental:
    - Recognize judgmental thoughts about yourself and others
    - Increase awareness of these thoughts
    - Label them as "just thoughts" without treating them as facts
- Be balanced in your thinking:
    - Acknowledge that difficulties arise from a combination of your own mistakes (and strengths), other people's mistakes (and strengths), and circumstances
    - Acknowledge both strengths and weaknesses

    - Be open about all sides of yourself
    - Share both your strengths and weaknesses with yourself and others
- Avoid definitive language:
    - Refrain from using terms like "always," "should," and "never"
    - Embrace the middle ground and acknowledge the nuances of reality
    - Replace definitive words with "often" or "sometimes" to reflect a more accurate perspective

Cultivating a Positive Self-Image

In our society, there is a strong emphasis on always wanting more. Simply being ourselves is often considered insufficient. We're constantly bombarded with messages that suggest we can improve ourselves or our lives by acquiring or achieving something new.

However, according to Scott Bea, a Doctor of Psychology, it is essential to recognize the importance of self-acceptance in order to truly accept who we are (Cleveland Clinic, 2020). To embrace our true selves, we must practice self-compassion and accept our inherent human nature. It's important to remember that having flaws doesn't make us inherently bad individuals.

Self-image is all about how we see ourselves—our thoughts, emotions, and beliefs about who we are as individuals. It encompasses our personality traits, abilities, and physical appearance (Shethna, 2023).

Many things contribute to our self-image, both from within us and from the world around us. Factors like genetics, life experiences, relationships, culture, and societal norms all play a role in shaping how we perceive ourselves.

I've curated ***12 ways you can cultivate your self-image.***

1. Stop criticizing yourself

- Avoid self-criticism for minor mistakes
- Embrace your imperfections and learn from them
- Practice self-forgiveness and focus on personal growth

2. Experience and express gratitude

- Practice gratitude journaling or activities
- Recognize your role in positive aspects of your life
- Foster a positive self-view through gratitude

3. Smile when you look in the mirror

- A simple smile can boost your self-image and confidence
- Even a fake smile can improve your mood
- Radiate positivity to others and yourself

4. Make a list of things you like about yourself

- Recognize and appreciate your positive qualities
- Include both small and significant aspects of yourself
- Boost your confidence and self-perception

5. Praise others liberally

- Acknowledge and praise the strengths and successes of others
- Celebrate the wellbeing and positive experiences of others
- Building others up contributes to a healthier self-image

6. Prioritize quality sleep

- Get enough sleep for a refreshed and positive mindset
- Adequate sleep improves mood, confidence, and focus
- Start the day with a positive self-image

7. Engage in activities you enjoy

- Pursue hobbies and interests that genuinely interest you
- Prioritize your own desires and passions
- Embrace new experiences to boost self-confidence

8. Have a plan for self-growth and enact it with determination

- Dedicate effort to personal growth and development
- Pursue activities for self-improvement
- Actively engage in actions that contribute to a positive self-image

9. Take social media breaks

- Temporarily disconnect from social media platforms
- Reduce social comparisons and negative self-perception
- Eliminate judgmental thoughts and foster a healthier self-image

10. Be authentic and true to yourself

- Embrace your unique qualities and personality
- Avoid trying to meet others' expectations of perfection
- Be comfortable in your own skin and let your true self shine

11. Dress in clothes that make you feel good

- Choose outfits that flatter your body and make you feel confident
- Prioritize comfort and personal style over trends
- Enhance your self-image through your fashion choices

12. Express yourself through hairstyles and/or makeup

- Experiment with hairstyles that make you feel good
- Wear makeup if it boosts your confidence and self-expression
- Embrace your personal style without worrying about others' opinions

Cultivating a positive self-image is an ongoing process that requires consistent effort and self-reflection. Resist hastiness. Allow yourself to grow and evolve over time.

Elements of Mindfulness

Non-judging

Cultivate a non-judgmental attitude towards yourself and others, letting go of critical thoughts and embracing acceptance.

Acceptance

Acknowledge and accept the present moment, including both the things within your control and those outside of it, to foster problem-solving and intentional living.

Patience

Embrace the understanding that personal growth and change take time, allowing yourself to experience the journey without rushing or forcing outcomes.

Beginner's mind

Approach each moment with curiosity and openness, seeing the world with fresh eyes and finding joy in the simple wonders of everyday life.

Trust

Develop trust in yourself by listening to your feelings and intuition, allowing them to guide your mindful awareness and decision-making.

Non-striving

Practice being present without striving for specific outcomes, observing and experiencing things without the need to constantly fix or achieve.

Letting go

Release attachments to past memories and future worries, observing and accepting your experiences in the present moment without clinging or aversion.

Gratitude

Cultivate an appreciation for the simple things in life, expressing thanks and acknowledging the positive aspects that contribute to happiness and wellbeing.

Generosity

Extend generosity towards yourself and others, offering gifts of time, acceptance, and support without expecting anything in return.

Mindfulness Self-Compassion Theory

Mindful self-compassion (MSC) is all about blending the skills you gain from mindfulness with the practice of being kind and compassionate toward yourself (Mead, 2019). It's a powerful combination that allows you to bring awareness to the present moment while also nurturing a sense of warmth and understanding toward yourself.

MSC helps you cultivate a compassionate attitude toward your own struggles and challenges, treating yourself with the same kindness and care you would offer to a close friend. By merging mindfulness and self-compassion, you can experience greater inner peace, resilience, and a greater capacity to navigate life's challenges with kindness and understanding.

Here are some practical MSC tools you can apply in your daily life:

Self-compassion break

- Pause during difficult moments.
- Acknowledge pain and suffering.
- Recognize shared humanity.
- Offer words of kindness and understanding to yourself.

Loving-kindness meditation

- Direct kindness to yourself and others.
- Extend well-wishes to loved ones, acquaintances, and even difficult individuals.

Self-compassion journaling

- Write down thoughts and emotions related to self-compassion.
- Reflect on self-criticism and challenging situations.
- Explore ways to offer yourself more compassion and develop a supportive inner dialogue.

Body scan meditation

- Bring mindful awareness to different parts of the body.
- Observe sensations and tensions without judgment.
- Cultivate connection and kindness towards your own body.

Informal mindfulness

- Incorporate mindfulness into your daily activities (e.g., brushing your teeth, eating, or taking a walk).
- Pay attention to the present moment.
- Approach tasks with a non-judgmental attitude.

P.S. You don't need to apply all of these tools. Just find the ones that resonate with you and make them a regular part of your life.

Mindfulness Exercises for Self-Compassion

1. Loving-kindness meditation

Spend a few minutes each day sending loving-kindness and compassion to yourself, using phrases like, "May I be happy, may I be healthy, may I be safe, may I live with ease."

2. Self-compassion break

When you're feeling stressed or struggling, take a moment to acknowledge your pain and offer yourself words of kindness and understanding. Remind yourself that suffering is part of being human.

3. Self-compassionate journaling

Write down your thoughts and feelings without judgment. Treat yourself with kindness and understanding as you reflect on your experiences.

4. Self-compassion affirmations

Create positive affirmations that promote self-compassion and repeat them to yourself regularly. Examples include, "I am worthy of love and compassion" or "I forgive myself for my mistakes."

5. Mindful walking

Take a mindful walk, paying attention to the sensation of each step, the movement of your body, and the sounds and sights around you. Practice self-compassion by offering yourself kind words as you walk.

6. Gratitude practice

Cultivate gratitude by focusing on the things you appreciate in your life. Each day, write down three things you're grateful for and reflect on why they bring you joy and gratitude.

7. Self-compassionate visualization

Imagine yourself in a peaceful and safe place where you feel loved and supported. Engage your senses to make the visualization vivid, and use it as a source of self-compassion.

8. Compassionate touch

Place your hand over your heart or give yourself a gentle hug to provide comfort and reassurance. Use touch as a physical reminder of self-compassion and care.

9. Self-compassionate letter

This exercise will help you cultivate self-compassion by offering yourself kind and supportive words, just as you would to a friend in need.

Instructions:

1. Think back to a time when you were overly harsh towards yourself or briefly felt inadequate or insecure.
2. Envision yourself composing a letter for a close friend who is experiencing similar circumstances.
3. Start the correspondence with "Dear [Your Name],".
4. Jot down the encouraging, kind, and understanding phrases you would typically use to comfort a friend. Treat yourself with compassion and patience, acknowledging your own difficulties.
5. Take your time and express compassion for yourself by writing as much as you need to.

Reflection:

Did it feel weird writing a compassionate letter to yourself? Did any insights come up during this exercise? Write down your reflections.

10. Self-compassion affirmations

This exercise will help you reinforce self-compassion by repeating positive affirmations that promote self-acceptance and kindness.

Instructions:

1. If possible, look at yourself in a mirror. If you don't have a mirror available, find a comfortable place where you can sit quietly.
2. Take a few deep breaths to center yourself.
3. Repeat the following affirmations out loud or in your mind:
    - I am deserving of love and compassion.
    - I accept myself as I am, flaws and all.
    - I am enough, just as I am at this moment.
    - I treat myself with kindness and understanding.
    - I am worthy of self-care and self-compassion.

4. Repeat each affirmation several times, allowing the words to sink in and resonate with you.

Reflection:

How did repeating the self-compassion affirmations make you feel? Did any particular affirmation resonate with you more than others? Write down your reflections.

11. Gratitude journaling

Another way to foster self-compassion is by focusing on the positive aspects of your life instead of the negatives and expressing gratitude for them.

Instructions:

1. Get a journal or some paper ready.
2. List three things in your life for which you are grateful at the moment, no matter small they might seem.
3. Think about how each of them makes you happy or brings you joy.
4. For each thing for which you are grateful, compose a little essay in which you express your gratitude and describe how it has improved your life.
5. If you're feeling inspired, continue writing in your journal about other aspects of your life that you're grateful for.

Reflection:

How did practicing gratitude make you feel? Did it shift your perspective and help you appreciate the present moment more, or are you still worried about all the bad things going on? Write down any reflections or insights.

Chapter Takeaway

The emphasis of this chapter has been on helping you live your life optimally without fear or any other negative emotions that make you hang your head in defeat.

Every exercise in this chapter is meant to help you cultivate self-compassion, self-acceptance, and mindfulness in your daily life. Feel free to modify them to suit your preferences and needs.

CHAPTER 4

The Self-Esteem Boost

"I praise you because I am fearfully and wonderfully made."

—Psalm 139:14

"If you hear a voice within you say 'you cannot paint,' then by all means paint, and that voice will be silenced."

—Vincent Van Gogh

Whenever I'm preparing to give a speech or write about the significance of self-esteem, I always remember a story Dr. Denny Coates, an expert in parent-child communication and author of several books including *Connect With Your Kid*, shared once about a young lad named Jason. I read the story long ago, but it has stuck with me.

Jason grew up in a large Christian family with parents who were good people. His dad served in the Navy, which meant he was often away from home, and his mom focused on taking care of the younger children. It was an environment where most kids would thrive, but Jason had a different path.

In high school, Jason played golf—and, boy, he was so good. Unfortunately, despite his talent, he constantly cheated during games. It wasn't just golf; he had a habit of lying about many things. His older brother, Mark, was an accomplished student, excelling in academics and popularity. Jason, on the other hand, seemed to feel bitter and inadequate compared to his brother.

Jason's actions only worsened his situation. He engaged in reckless behavior like starting a forest fire, getting caught shoplifting, and damaging the family car. Graduation day was marked by a destructive outburst, symbolizing his anger and desire for approval that he didn't receive. His low self-esteem fueled a destructive cycle.

Jason grew malicious and highly temperamental. He later enlisted in the Navy, but his struggles with alcoholism led to a Dishonorable Discharge. He became an outcast in his own family after seducing his younger brother's wife and was tragically gunned down in Miami.

Don't forget that Jason started out a talented golfer, but he didn't focus on that; rather, he allowed the successes of others to define his life—a symptom of low self-worth—leading to destructive choices.

"WOOOH! I'm awesome! ...Although I do believe I left my keys in the car."

Are You Your Worst Critic?

Why do you do that to yourself?

Why do you put the blame on yourself whenever you feel inadequate?

Yes, it's important to have high standards and strive towards your goals and dreams. But sometimes, these self-imposed expectations can backfire and lead you to criticize yourself harshly. Without realizing it, you become your own worst critic, constantly belittling yourself with negative self-talk (Nasir, 2019).

For those with low self-esteem, our entire world exists within the bubble we have created for ourselves. In this bubble, we hold ourselves to an immeasurable standard of perfection. When that standard fails to be met, our carefully crafted image begins to crumble, piece by piece. It feels like the world is collapsing around us, and we start questioning our worth.

We replay scenarios, imagining different outcomes, and negative thoughts like "I'm not good enough" spiral in our heads. This self-deprecating dialogue tears us down and sabotages our progress, stripping us of our self-esteem.

Here's the thing: the standards by which we measure ourselves, our self-worth, and our value are not even real. We created them ourselves. These benchmarks that we desperately want to attain, that feel like a matter of life or death, were created by us.

But what happens when we believe these self-imposed labels and standards?

- We make heartache, regret, and disappointment a norm in our lives.
- We feel undeserving and unworthy, constantly seeking approval from others.
- We try to prove ourselves to the world, desperately grasping at any form of flattery to feel good.

- We fear being exposed as flawed and believe our failures are the logical outcome of who we really are.
- The self-critiquing and hatefulness we carry within ourselves erode our self-esteem, robbing us of joy and self-acceptance.

While others may see our successes and accomplishments, we struggle to believe in ourselves. We attribute our achievements to luck or chance because we don't truly believe we have the power to make great things happen. We become our own worst critic, doubting our abilities and undermining our self-worth.

It's time to break free from this cycle and cultivate a healthier self-image.

- You have the power to shape your self-worth and define your own standards.
- Mistakes and setbacks do not define you; they are opportunities for growth.
- Focus on your strengths and celebrate your achievements, no matter how small.
- Surround yourself with positive influences and supportive people who uplift you.
- Practice self-compassion and kindness towards yourself, replacing self-criticism with self-love.

Recognizing and Addressing Negative Self-Talk

Everyone has experienced that inner critic, the little voice that offers critiques of what we're doing (Scott, 2022b). Sometimes it can actually be useful, like when it nudges us to make healthier choices or think twice before doing something risky.

But can I be real with you? That little voice can also be a real pain. It starts whispering all these negative things, and before we know it, we're trapped in a spiral of self-doubt and self-criticism. Yeah, it's called negative self-talk, and it's a real mood killer.

The Mayo Clinic (2022) identifies different forms of negative self-talk, including:

1. **Filtering:** This happens when we focus solely on the negative aspects of a situation and disregard any positive elements (e.g., ignoring a productive day at work and compliments from coworkers and choosing to dwell on unfinished tasks).
2. **Personalizing:** This involves blaming ourselves for things that aren't our fault (e.g., assuming that plans with friends got canceled because nobody wanted to be around us).
3. **Catastrophizing:** This is the tendency to anticipate the worst-case scenario without any supporting evidence (e.g., receiving an incorrect drive-through order and

immediately beginning to catastrophize, believing the rest of the day will be an absolute disaster).

4. **Blaming:** Instead of taking responsibility, we shift the blame onto others. We fail to acknowledge our own role and attribute our experiences to external factors.
5. **"Should" statements:** This refers to constantly imposing unrealistic expectations on ourselves. We repeatedly remind ourselves of all the things we "should" be doing, which leads to feelings of guilt and inadequacy.
6. **Magnifying:** This occurs when we blow minor problems out of proportion, making them seem much bigger than they actually are. It amplifies stress and creates unnecessary distress.
7. **Perfectionism:** This is setting unattainable standards for ourselves. Striving for flawlessness leads to constant disappointment and a sense of failure.
8. **Polarizing:** This refers to viewing things in absolute terms, without considering any middle ground. It's a rigid thinking pattern where situations are either completely good or completely bad, leaving no room for nuance.

How to Address Negative Self-Talk

Become aware of it

- Take a time out to reflect on your thoughts and inner voice.
- Try journaling to improve your awareness of negative thinking.

Challenge negative self-talk

- Recognize negative thinking patterns and challenge irrational beliefs.
- Use positive affirmations to retrain your mind and shift your perspective.

Practice positive self-talk

- Focus on your blessings and shift your attention to the positive.
- Practice gratitude through reflection, thankfulness, or a gratitude journal.

Step outside of yourself

- Shift perspectives by asking how your best friend would view the situation.
- Develop self-talk rooted in self-love and compassion.

Talk it out

- Seek support from loved ones or a therapist to challenge negativity.
- Discuss your thoughts to gain clarity and separate reality from negative thinking.

Put it on the shelf

- When negative thoughts become overwhelming, visualize setting them aside.
- Revisit those thoughts at a later time that better serves you.

Focus on the present moment

- Practice mindfulness techniques to refocus your mind and break free from negative thoughts.
- Engage in breathing exercises, grounding, or meditation to stay present and find relief.

Self-Criticism and Your Self-Esteem

Self-criticism and self-esteem are two interconnected aspects of our self-perception and inner dialogue.

Sometimes, without even realizing it, we carry around a sense of discomfort within ourselves. We have a habit of criticizing our own thoughts, feelings, and actions before anyone else gets the chance to criticize us. This is a manifestation of low self-esteem (Gilbertson, 2010). It stems from past experiences where we felt unworthy, and it continues to affect us through a never-ending cycle of self-criticism.

Self-criticism can be fueled by negative self-talk, where we engage in a constant stream of self-deprecating thoughts. It can hinder our progress, diminish our self-confidence, and create a cycle of negativity and self-doubt.

Balancing self-criticism and self-esteem

1. It's important to find a balance between self-criticism and self-esteem to foster personal growth without falling into a pattern of excessive negativity.
2. Acknowledge areas for improvement without harshly judging yourself, and use self-criticism as a constructive tool rather than a source of self-sabotage.
3. Cultivate self-compassion and supportive inner dialogue, treating yourself with kindness and understanding during challenging times.
4. Practice self-reflection and self-awareness to recognize when self-criticism becomes excessive, and consciously shift your focus towards nurturing self-esteem.

Exploring Possible Causes of Low Self-Esteem

In the first part of this book, I listed numerous things that cause low self-esteem. In this part, however, I'll focus on a few of these and expound on them.

1. Authority figures in conflict

- Witnessing parents or caregivers engage in constant conflict can make a child feel scared, overwhelmed, and responsible for their pain.
- These intense conflicts can create a sense of being "tainted" or to blame, leading to low self-esteem that may persist into adulthood.

2. Bullying

- Experiencing bullying can leave lasting emotional scars, especially if there is a lack of support from a safe and responsive family environment.
- Bullying can make a child feel undeserving of attention and abandoned, and eventually develop a sense of self-loathing.
- In the absence of a supportive home life, the effects of bullying can continue to impact self-esteem well into adulthood.

3. Academic challenges

- Struggling with academics and feeling incapable of understanding classroom material can deeply impact self-esteem.
- Falling behind without support or intervention can lead to feelings of inadequacy and internalization of a belief in one's own lack of intelligence.
- Challenged learners may become excessively self-conscious about sharing thoughts and opinions, doubting their own intelligence and abilities.

4. Trauma

- Experiencing physical, sexual, or emotional abuse can profoundly affect self-esteem.
- Victims may struggle with displaced guilt and blame themselves, leading to deep shame and self-loathing.
- Difficulty trusting others due to trauma can further contribute to low self-esteem.

5. Society and the media

- Unrealistic standards of physical beauty perpetuated by media images and depictions can negatively impact self-esteem.

- Exposure to unfair physical comparisons from a young age can lead to negative self-image and the development of eating disorders.
- Feeling inadequate based on societal and materialistic standards can have long-lasting effects on self-esteem into adulthood.

Developing a Healthy Sense of Worth

Self-worth plays a significant role in many aspects of our lives. Among other things, it influences our relationships, work performance, self-perception, and even how others perceive us (Gupta, 2023).

According to Sabrina Romanoff, PsyD, a clinical psychologist and professor at Yeshiva University (cited by Gupta, 2023), self-worth is a subjective concept that can be influenced by various factors. These factors include core beliefs and values, thoughts and feelings, emotions and mental wellbeing, experiences and interactions with others, relationships, health and physical fitness, career and profession, activities and hobbies, community and social status, financial position, and physical appearance.

All of these aspects can have an impact on how individuals perceive and assess their own self-worth.

Here are some strategies suggested by Dr. Romanoff to enhance your self-worth (cited by Gupta, 2023):

1. Engage in activities you enjoy and excel at

Finding activities that bring you joy and allow you to showcase your skills can boost your self-worth. Recognizing your talents and strengths reinforces feelings of competence and confidence, which can positively impact other areas of your life.

2. Embrace challenges and push your limits

Research indicates that physical exercise is linked to higher self-worth. By challenging yourself physically and setting progressively more ambitious goals, you can demonstrate your capabilities and expand your belief in your own potential. Exercise also has the added benefit of improving your mental wellbeing.

3. Challenge negative thoughts

Remember that your thoughts are not always accurate reflections of reality. Negative self-talk often arises from internalized criticism, stress, or external pressures. Whenever you catch yourself engaging in negative self-talk, try replacing those thoughts with more realistic and positive alternatives.

4. Seek support

If you find that low self-worth is impacting your relationships, work, or overall emotional wellbeing, it may be beneficial to seek the guidance of a therapist. Low self-worth can limit your perspective and lead to complacency, making it crucial to seek professional help to overcome these challenges. A therapist can offer a neutral perspective and provide effective strategies for building self-worth.

Mindful Strategies to Boost Your Self-Esteem

Rachael Kable, host of The Mindful Kind podcast, shares some mindfulness strategies you can apply to boost your self-esteem. Below is a summary of her practical tips, which you can read more about on her blog (Kable, 2016):

1. Be your own supporter

Instead of seeking validation from others, take time to reflect on your worthiness. Make a list of your positive qualities, from acts of kindness to traits you appreciate about yourself. Embrace and believe in these attributes wholeheartedly.

2. Practice positive self-talk

Whenever you consciously choose to believe in yourself and acknowledge your efforts, reward yourself. Commend yourself for recognizing your own abilities and doing your best.

3. Engage in activities that uplift your mood

When facing a tough day or pursuing your dreams, remind yourself that it's temporary and take a break to boost your spirits. Listen to uplifting music, visit your favorite restaurant, spend time with loved ones or pets, participate in rejuvenating activities or self-care—do whatever brings you joy and makes you feel good.

4. Step outside your comfort zone gradually

If public speaking terrifies you, for example, don't rush into speaking in front of large audiences right away. Take small steps to build your confidence. You could start by creating a podcast, then practice speaking in front of family members, and gradually work your way up to speaking at events. After each step, practice self-care to reinforce feelings of safety and security, strengthening your confidence for the next challenge.

5. Practice mindfulness when overwhelmed

Stress, fear, and overwhelm can undermine your confidence. When you notice your confidence wavering due to these emotions, practice mindfulness techniques to regain calm, focus, and clarity. This can include breathing exercises, mindful walks, or engaging your senses by noticing things around you.

6. Embrace confidence without fear

Many people mistake confidence for arrogance and feel afraid of appearing overly confident, but these are two different things. Confidence inspires others and fosters a positive environment, while arrogance is intimidating and drains the confidence of those around you. Confidence is genuine and open to feedback, while arrogance often stems from insecurity seeking external validation.

7. Practice kindness

Kindness is a powerful confidence booster. When you choose to be kind to others, it not only benefits them but also enhances your own confidence. You can show kindness by simply smiling at others, actively listening, or reaching out to loved ones to check in on them.

8. Believe in your own confidence

It's crucial to see yourself as a confident person. If you continue to tell yourself that you lack confidence, it becomes a self-fulfilling prophecy. Challenge your self-perception by asking yourself what actions you can take to strengthen your self-belief and which thoughts you need to change to genuinely embrace your confidence.

Chapter Takeaway

The primary focus of this chapter is to prod you to shift your gaze from the negativity that seems to engulf your mind and help you recognize the goodness locked within you.

Until you begin to say some really nice, positive things to yourself, you won't be able to attempt anything great in life. You'll be a shadow of yourself and live in mediocrity, trapped by lack of self-worth.

Before you allow your imagination and negative thoughts to consume you and sentence you to a life of unhappiness, dare to practice the mindfulness skills that have been recommended in this chapter to gradually step out of that dark box of low self-esteem.

P.S As you continue your voyage through these pages of discovery, we invite you to share your thoughts, feeling, and impressions with us. That will illuminate the path of all seekers of knowledge.

Before you venture into the next chapter, we encourage you to **pen down your impressions below.** Your contributions breathe life into the ongoing dialog and inspire fellow seekers of knowledge,

Thank you for being part of this journey.

With appreciation,

Click **HERE** to leave your review! Or Scan the QR CODE

CHAPTER 5

Your Emotional Health

"He heals the broken hearted and binds up their wounds."

—Psalms 147:3

"When our emotional health is in a bad state, so is our level of self-esteem. We have to slow down and deal with what is troubling us so that we can enjoy the simple joy of being happy and at peace with ourselves."

—Jess C. Scott

At 16 years old, Alex seemed to have it all together. He excelled in school, had a supportive group of friends, and participated in various activities. From the outside, everything seemed perfect, but deep down, Alex was struggling with his emotional health.

Alex often felt overwhelmed by the pressure to succeed and meet everyone's expectations. He put on a brave face, but inside, a whirlwind of emotions was brewing. Anxiety, self-doubt, and sadness frequently crept in, leaving him feeling trapped and confused.

This continued until Alex mustered the courage to reach out for help. When he finally talked to one of his trusted friends, he realized he wasn't the only one with emotional struggles. Together, they started researching and discovered the power of self-care, mindfulness, and self-compassion. Alex and his friend began implementing small changes in their daily routine. They set aside time each day to practice mindfulness exercises, like journaling their thoughts and feelings. They also made sure to engage in activities they enjoyed, such as painting, playing an instrument, or going for walks in nature.

As time went on, Alex and his friend noticed a positive shift in their emotional health. They started to understand that it was okay to prioritize their wellbeing and that their worth wasn't solely based on external achievements.

With newfound tools and a support system, Alex continued to navigate the ups and downs of life with a greater sense of emotional balance.

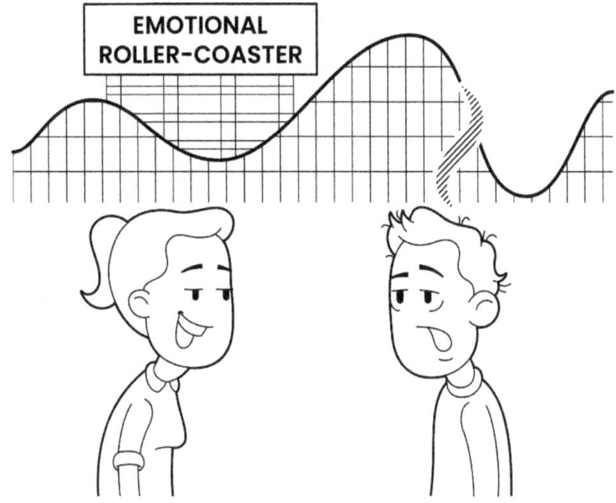

"You were right - that was a terrible idea."

The Complexity of Our Emotions

Emotional complexity refers to the way we understand and handle our emotions. It's about our ability to tell the difference between pleasant and unpleasant feelings and how we see them in relation to each other. Everyone has their own unique way of dealing with emotions and figuring out what makes them feel good or bad (Ong & Bergeman, 2004).

Someone who is "emotionally complex" might have a unique ability to see both the positive and negative aspects of situations. They can describe their feelings in great detail and accuracy, and they're able to predict which emotions will arise in different circumstances. They can remember experiencing multiple emotions simultaneously.

However, that's just one description of this term. The concept of emotional complexity is quite diverse and can be understood in various ways within the field of psychology—meaning that there are numerous ways a person can be considered "emotionally complex."

Dr. Colleen Cira (cited by Hill, 2021), a clinical psychologist, notes that when we talk about emotional complexity, it's like saying someone is a bit of a puzzle when it comes to their feelings, thoughts, behavior, or reactions; it's not easy to predict how they will respond in different situations.

Before we delve into this further, here are some key facts about human emotion:

- Our emotions are fascinating and complex aspects of being human.
- Emotions go beyond simple black-and-white categories and exist on a spectrum.
- Emotions can be influenced by various factors, such as our experiences and circumstances.
- We can feel multiple emotions simultaneously or have conflicting emotions about a situation.
- Emotional complexity involves the ability to identify, understand, and express a range of diverse emotions.
- Some individuals have a higher level of emotional awareness and can articulate their feelings with precision.

- Developing emotional intelligence through self-reflection, mindfulness, and connections with others can enhance our understanding and management of our emotions.

Understanding Your Emotional Health

Emotional wellbeing encompasses our thoughts and emotions, reflecting our overall state of being. It involves our capacity to navigate life's challenges, acknowledge and manage our own emotions, as well as empathize with others. It's important to note that emotional wellbeing is not synonymous with constant happiness (Miller, 2020).

Being emotionally healthy means having the ability to accept and effectively handle our feelings, even in the face of adversity and change. It entails being able to process and understand our emotions in a constructive manner, promoting a balanced and healthy mindset.

Brennan (2021) adds that emotional health is a part of mental wellbeing. It's all about being aware of your emotions, both the good and the bad, and how you handle them. When it comes to negative emotions, emotionally healthy individuals have effective coping strategies in place and also recognize when it's necessary to seek professional support.

The following are the qualities of an emotionally healthy life:

1. **Self-awareness:** An emotionally healthy person has the ability to recognize and redirect their emotions when necessary to navigate both distress and elation. This skill develops throughout childhood but can be strengthened in adulthood through practice.

2. **Self-acceptance:** Emotionally healthy individuals accept themselves and are capable of handling adversity with clarity. They might allow themselves space to express and process emotions, such as having a "behind closed doors" temper tantrum to release anger in a healthy way.

3. **Self-care:** Those with good emotional health prioritize self-compassion and take care of their physical wellbeing. They intentionally and regularly practice self-care to ensure their overall wellbeing.

4. **Emotional agility:** An emotionally healthy person is not immune to setbacks or adversity. However, with an open mind and a curious thought process, they have the ability to thrive through difficulties and adapt to challenging circumstances.

5. **Coping skills:** Emotionally healthy individuals possess strong coping skills. By practicing these skills during calm times, they build resilience, which helps them navigate turbulent periods. It's like preparing for

battle—adversity is inevitable in real life, and emotional capital is built during peaceful moments.

6. **Kindness and integrity:** An emotionally healthy person treats others with kindness and integrity, without expecting anything in return. They approach interactions with curiosity and compassion, fostering positive connections with those around them.
7. **Living with purpose:** Having a sense of purpose is another characteristic of an emotionally healthy person. They focus less on their inner experiences and more on how their experiences can serve others. They acknowledge their emotions but prioritize the bigger picture, allowing emotions to pass and embracing their purpose.
8. **Stress management and serenity:** An emotionally healthy person manages stress effectively and regularly practices moments of serenity. Just as good leaders remain calm during chaotic circumstances, self-mastery requires the same ability to find inner peace amidst external challenges.

You're most likely unhealthy emotionally (and could also be dealing with a mental illness, such as depression) if you consistently experience the following:

- Social isolation from friends, family, or coworkers

- Neglecting personal hygiene and self-care routines
- Decreased energy levels
- Disrupted sleep patterns, either excessive or insufficient
- Changes in appetite, either overeating or undereating
- Increased reliance on substances
- Racing thoughts
- Heightened interpersonal conflicts
- Feelings of irritability, guilt, hopelessness, or worthlessness
- A decline in work performance or productivity

Create an Emotional Reset

There is a powerful tool you can use when you're feeling overwhelmed by stress and anxiety. It's called the Emotional Reset Technique, or ERT, and it was created by therapist and author Jacqui Olliver (Olliver, 2023).

Whenever you're faced with overwhelming feelings or triggers, this amazing method comes to the rescue, preventing your mind from getting trapped in a whirlwind of thoughts and overthinking. Instead, it empowers you to shift your focus and regain control over your emotions.

By doing so, you can foster a sense of inner calm and clarity, allowing you to communicate more confidently and say goodbye to mental turmoil. Hereprocess simple five-step emotional reset process that can help you connect with your emotions:

Step 1: Pause and take three deep breaths, consciously allowing your body to relax. Release any tension you feel, letting each breath loosen your muscles.

Step 2: Ask yourself, "What am I feeling right now?" Embrace the emotion and fully experience it. Are you feeling sadness, happiness, resentment, gratitude, loneliness, excitement, frustration, peace…?

Step 3: Let go of any negative self-talk that arises. As you continue to breathe, practice self-acceptance. Inhale acceptance, exhale judgment. Inhale peace, exhale stress.

Step 4: Reflect on how you want to feel. It's okay if you're not ready to let go of your current emotions just yet. You may need to fully experience your anger or sadness before moving forward. Remember, whatever you feel is valid and okay. When you're ready, ask yourself again how you want to feel.

Step 5: Take a proactive step towards improving your emotional state. If you're feeling lonely, consider reaching out to a friend for a meaningful conversation or engage in self-care at home. If you're harboring resentment, have a calm conversation with the person involved and express your need for a positive change. Take action aligned with how you want to feel.

Understanding Emotional Regulation

According to Thompson (1994), emotional regulation involves both internal and external processes, including monitoring, evaluating, and adjusting our emotional responses to achieve our goals. Gross (1998) defines emotional regulation as the way we influence and express the emotions we experience. Additionally, a crucial part of emotional regulation is aligning with societal expectations and our own needs (Cole, Michel, & Teti, 1994).

Lebow and Casabianca (2022) provide perhaps a simpler definition: emotional regulation refers to the skill of recognizing, controlling, and effectively dealing with your emotions. It plays a crucial role in how you interact with yourself, others, and the world around you. Without proper regulation, emotions can easily take control and affect various aspects of your life.

Emotional regulation is a skill that we must learn and develop, and it is a fundamental aspect of emotional intelligence. It involves being able to process information, maintain a composed response that aligns with the situation, and effectively communicate our needs to others.

Practicing emotional regulation requires creating a sacred space between experiencing an emotion and reacting to it. It could mean taking a pause to gather your thoughts before responding.

It can also involve waiting until you are in a supportive environment before you begin processing difficult emotions.

Emotional regulation is essential for overall mental wellbeing and for establishing healthy relationships. When we master this skill, it empowers us to:

- Maintain a sense of balance and control over our emotional reactions
- Stay composed and calm in challenging situations
- Effectively manage and cope with stress
- Preserve and nurture important relationships
- Actively listen to and understand the needs of others
- Express our own needs in a constructive manner
- Demonstrate professionalism in work-related situations
- Avoid taking things personally and maintain objectivity

The Three Emotional Regulation Systems

According to Gilbert's theory, our emotional system can be divided into three parts that interact with each other. These systems play a role in mental health issues.

1. The first system is focused on threat and self-protection. It reacts to signs of danger and triggers negative emotions like anxiety, anger, and disgust. Its purpose is to keep us safe from threats and harm.

2. The second system is focused on drive-seeking and acquisition. It drives us to seek resources necessary for survival and reproduction. It responds to signs of reward and generates positive emotions such as vitality and excitement. However, excessive activation of this system can lead to a constant search for resources and increase the risk of mental health problems.
3. The third system is focused on soothing behaviors. It is connected to our attachment system and aims to suppress the threat and drive systems, creating a sense of calm and safety. It responds to signs of warmth and affiliation, leading to positive emotions like calmness, contentment, and feelings of social connection.

Emotional Regulation and Self-Compassion: The Interrelation

Emotional regulation and self-compassion are closely interconnected and play a significant role in our wellbeing and mental health.

Emotional regulation, as we have discussed, refers to the ability to recognize, understand, and manage our emotions. Self-compassion, on the other hand, involves treating ourselves with kindness, understanding, and acceptance, especially in times of difficulty or failure. It entails being supportive and nurturing toward ourselves, just as we would be toward a close friend or loved one. Self-compassion allows us to acknowledge our pain and suffering without judgment or self-criticism.

The interrelationship between emotional regulation and self-compassion becomes apparent when we consider how they influence each other:

1. **Emotional regulation enhances self-compassion:** When we develop effective emotional regulation skills, we can respond to our emotions with compassion and understanding. Instead of being overwhelmed or harshly judging ourselves for experiencing certain emotions, we can approach ourselves with kindness and self-care.
2. **Self-compassion supports emotional regulation:** Practicing self-compassion provides a nurturing and safe space to explore and regulate our emotions. By accepting our emotions without judgment, we can better understand their underlying causes and respond to them in a healthy and constructive manner.
3. **Both contribute to overall wellbeing:** Emotional regulation and self-compassion are vital for promoting mental health and wellbeing. When we regulate our emotions effectively and show ourselves compassion, we cultivate emotional balance, reduce stress, and foster resilience.

Compassion Focused Therapy

Compassion focused therapy (CFT) was created by Paul Gilbert, a professor of clinical psychology, to help people deal with mental health issues involving feelings of shame or self-blame. It's specifically designed for those who find it hard to connect their thoughts with their emotions, which is often called "head-heart lag" (Lee, 2005; Stott, 2007).

In CFT, the focus is on developing compassion for oneself and others. The therapy aims to help individuals cultivate a kinder and more understanding attitude toward themselves, especially during tough times. It encourages people to acknowledge their struggles without judgment and to treat themselves with care and kindness (Alavi, 2021).

The goal of CFT is to bridge the gap between knowing something logically and truly feeling it deep inside. It helps individuals develop a sense of emotional connection and empathy towards themselves and others, leading to greater emotional wellbeing and improved mental health.

CFT is a valuable approach for anyone who finds it challenging to show themselves compassion or who tends to be self-critical. By learning to be kinder to yourself and developing a compassionate mindset, you can find relief from shame, self-attack, and self-blame, and move towards a healthier and more balanced mental state.

How does CFT work?

Compassion focused therapy is based on the idea that our brain has three different systems that help us survive and feel good.

These systems developed a long time ago and still affect how we feel, act, and think today.

1. **Threat system:** This system helps us sense and respond to threats. When we encounter something scary or dangerous, we might feel fear, anxiety, or anger. Our body may react by wanting to fight, run away, or freeze. Sometimes we may also experience biased thoughts or jump to conclusions when we feel threatened.
2. **Drive system:** The drive system is all about pursuing important goals and finding resources. It gives us motivation and pleasure when we achieve something we want. However, if this system becomes too strong, it can lead to risky behaviors like using drugs and alcohol.
3. **Contentment system:** This system is connected to feelings of happiness and calm. It's not just about seeking pleasure or avoiding threats, but about feeling connected to others, cared for, and safe. The contentment system helps regulate the threat and drive systems, keeping them in balance.

CFT techniques and exercises

In CFT, therapists use a variety of techniques to help clients develop compassion for themselves and others. Here are some common ones:

1. **Appreciation exercises:** These activities focus on the things that bring you joy and pleasure. You might make a list of things you like, take time to enjoy the moment when something good happens, or engage in positive, rewarding behaviors.
2. **Mindfulness:** This is about paying attention to the present moment without judging it. It helps you become aware of your thoughts, feelings, and sensations in a non-judgmental way.
3. **Compassion-focused imagery exercises:** These exercises use guided memories and fantasies to create a mental image that stimulates the contentment system. The goal is to evoke feelings of warmth, safety, and care.
4. **Exploring self-attacks:** If you struggle with self-criticism, the therapist can help you understand why it happens and where it comes from. They might ask you to visualize your self-attacking thoughts as a person and describe what that person looks like and how they make you feel. This helps you better understand and address your self-criticism.
5. **Developing compassion:** If you find it hard to show compassion to yourself or others, the therapist will ask you questions to explore any barriers or reasons why it might be difficult for you. They can help you work

through these blockages and find ways to express compassion.

CFT Worksheet

Emotion Carousel

Instructions:

1. Spend a moment getting comfy before getting ready to examine the complex tapestry of your emotions.
2. Think about the feelings stated below. Write down one emotion that is very important to you at this time and write it down.

Emotions to choose from:

- Joy
- Anger
- Sadness
- Fear
- Excitement
- Guilt
- Disgust
- Surprise
- Anxiety
- Love

3. Complete each section based on the prompts given, allowing your creativity to shine.

4. Remember, this exercise is a gentle exploration of your emotions, fostering self-compassion and growth.

Emotion Carousel Worksheet:

1. Emotion: ________________________________

2. Word Association:

Take a moment to reflect on your chosen emotion. Write down five words or phrases that come to mind when you think of this emotion, and write those words down.

a. ____

b. ____

c. ____

d. ____

e. ____

3. Physical Sensations:

Take a breather and pay attention to your body. What bodily sensations do you experience when you have this feeling (tingling, sweating, etc.)? Please explain in the space provided.

____

____

____

4. Triggers:

Examine the various situations, occasions, or ideas that usually cause you to feel this way. Spend some time writing down or elaborating on some examples.

____

____

5. Cultivating Self-Compassion:

Think of yourself as a close friend who is presently experiencing this. What comforting and motivating things would you say to them? Fill the space below with the comforting words you'd say.

____

____

6. Perspective Shift:

Let's examine a few alternative viewpoints on this feeling that can be empowering or lead to a positive shift. Write down a fresh perspective or an affirming statement that can help reframe this emotion for you.

____

____

____

7. Healthy Coping Strategies:

List three effective coping or management techniques for this feeling as it arises. Any relaxing activities are acceptable as part of these strategies.

a. ____

b. ____

c. ____

8. Gratitude:

Specify a feature of this emotion for which you are grateful. It might be a chance to learn something valuable, advance personally, or develop stronger relationships. Write it down below.

____

____

9. Reflection:

Take a moment to reflect on the insights you've made about yourself and this emotion throughout this exercise. Are there any action steps you'd like to embrace moving forward? Write them below.

____

____

Chapter Takeaway

Taking care of your mental health is crucial for your overall wellbeing. By practicing mindfulness techniques, learning emotional regulation skills, and exploring compassion focused therapy (CFT), you can effectively manage negative emotions and reduce stress and anxiety.

These tools are valuable resources that can significantly improve your mental wellbeing. Don't hesitate to explore and embrace them to nurture your mind and live a happier, healthier life.

CHAPTER 6

Dealing with Depression

"The Lord is close to the brokenhearted and saves those who are crushed in spirit."

—Psalms 34:18

"A big part of depression is feeling really lonely, even if you're in a room full of a million people."

—Lilly Singh

A Wandering Mind and Depression

Have you ever caught yourself daydreaming and noticed that your thoughts tend to lean toward the negative? It's common to think about the future or remember past events, but sometimes those thoughts can become a bit gloomy.

Scientists are still trying to unravel the mysteries of our thoughts and how they shape our consciousness. One interesting aspect they're studying is the tendency for negative thoughts to cycle and repeat in our minds (Seth, 2018). Understanding this pattern could give us valuable insights into mental health.

So, the next time you find yourself lost in your thoughts, pay attention to whether they tend to be more negative or positive. It's an important clue that can help you better understand your mind and how you can cultivate a healthier thought process.

There's a lot of research out there about how overthinking and dwelling on negative thoughts can contribute to feelings of sadness and depression. But when it comes to simply letting our minds wander, there's not as much information available (Chaieb et al., 2022).

So, here's the thing: we're not quite sure yet if the way our minds wander is different when we're feeling down or depressed. And if there are differences, we're still trying to figure out how they're connected to those repetitive negative thoughts. It's an open question that researchers are still exploring.

But ***what is a wandering mind?***

A wandering mind is when your thoughts start drifting away from what you're supposed to be focusing on and into unrelated stuff. It's like your mind decides to take a little detour and think about things that don't really matter in that moment (Smallwood & Schooler, 2006).

Research has shown that a wandering mind is not a happy mind. In a study conducted by Matthew Killingsworth and Daniel Gilbert, it was found that almost half of the time, people's thoughts were focused on something other than what they were currently doing. Interestingly, it didn't matter whether these thoughts were positive or negative; the more time people spent thinking about things unrelated to the present moment, the more unhappy they felt (Killingsworth & Gilbert, 2010).

With a growing number of people experiencing depression and other mood disorders, it becomes important for us to learn ways to interrupt and redirect our wandering minds. By doing so, we can improve our overall happiness and wellbeing.

"OK. All downhill from here!"

How Depression Influences the Body-Mind Connection

Depression affects more than just your mood. It can also have physical symptoms. Here are a few of the most common:

- Increased aches and pains: Approximately two out of three people with depression experience increased physical pain.
- Chronic fatigue: Feeling constantly tired and lacking energy is a common symptom.
- Decreased appetite: Many people with depression experience a decrease in their appetite and may have difficulty eating.
- Sleep disturbances: Insomnia, difficulty sleeping deeply, or oversleeping are common sleep problems associated with depression.

But what causes these physical symptoms of depression? Changes in the brain can have an impact on various systems in the body. For example, abnormal functioning of neurotransmitters like serotonin, which affects mood, can also influence pain perception. This means that you may become more sensitive to pain, especially back pain. Serotonin also plays a role in sleep and sexual drive, and it's not uncommon for individuals with depression to experience difficulties in these areas.

Unfortunately, the physical symptoms of depression are often overlooked by those suffering from depression, their families, and even healthcare professionals. In spite of the fact that sleep problems, fatigue, and concerns about health have been found to be reliable indicators of depression in some older adults, these signs are often dismissed as a natural part of aging.

It's important to note that depression also increases your risk of developing other physical illnesses. It can raise levels of stress hormones like cortisol and adrenaline, which have negative effects on the body over prolonged periods. It can weaken the immune system, making it harder for your body to fight infections.

Additionally, some vaccinations, such as the shingles vaccine, may be less effective in older adults with depression. Depression has also been linked to heart disease and an increased risk of substance abuse.

The physical changes caused by depression, such as sleep disturbances or a weakened immune system, can worsen existing illnesses as well. Similarly, physical changes caused by chronic diseases or depression itself can trigger or worsen depressive symptoms.

This creates a cycle that can be challenging to break without proper treatment for both depression and any other coexisting medical conditions. It's important to address both aspects to improve overall wellbeing and break the cycle.*

*Boost your Mental Health with Worksheet #6. Download the **BONUS** to check it out.

Detaching for a Happier Life

Sometimes, we get really attached to things, goals, dreams, or even people. We feel like if we don't have them, we won't be complete. This attachment can bring up all sorts of emotions like anxiety, fear, anger, jealousy, and sadness. It can make us feel disconnected from ourselves and others. But here's the thing: we don't need to be attached to anything to be whole.

Attachments can be to relationships, money, social status, or even our jobs. We use these things to define ourselves and who we are. But the truth is, we are more than just those labels. If something changes or we lose something we're attached to, it doesn't change who we are deep down.

So how do we let go of unhealthy attachments? Here are five steps to help:

1. **Pay attention to your thoughts:** Notice the thoughts that come up regularly. What labels do you identify with the most? This awareness can help you understand where your attachments lie. Attachments often come with strong emotions, so pay attention to how your body feels when you think about them.
2. **Separate your ego from reality:** Sometimes our ego makes us believe that not getting something we want is the end of the world. But the reality is, it's just a disappointment. The situation hasn't changed, only

our thoughts about it. You can still move forward and achieve your goals.

3. **Embrace uncertainty:** Security doesn't come from holding on to things. It comes from accepting the unknown and being open to new possibilities. Let go of the need for certainty, and you'll find true happiness and fulfillment.

4. **Try meditation:** Meditation is a great way to quiet your mind and let go of old thought patterns that no longer serve you. Spend some time each day in meditation and you'll start to see positive changes in your life.

5. **Be kind to yourself:** Changing old habits takes time and effort. Instead of being hard on yourself when you slip back into old patterns, celebrate the fact that you're aware of them. Awareness is the first step toward transformation.

Self-Compassion and Depression

It can be tough to show yourself kindness and compassion when you're dealing with depression, but making some small changes can actually make a big difference in how you feel.

Here's the thing: nobody is perfect. We all have our own quirks, flaws, and complexities. Compassion helps us show kindness and forgiveness to others, but somehow, we often forget to treat ourselves with the same understanding.

So, the first step to practicing self-compassion is to recognize that you're human, just like everyone else. It's okay to struggle, and even though it may not always come naturally, you deserve your own compassion and understanding.

1. Remember, depression isn't your fault

When you're living with depression, it's easy to blame yourself and wonder why you can't just be happier. But here's the truth: Depression is not a choice you make. You're not waking up each day and deciding to feel down or isolated. It's important to practice self-compassion and remind yourself that you're not to blame for your depression symptoms.

2. Change your perspective

When practicing mindfulness while dealing with depression, try shifting your perspective. Instead of being hard on yourself, imagine you're talking to a friend going through the same situation. You wouldn't say harsh things to them, so why say them to yourself? Changing your perspective can help you be kinder and more understanding towards yourself.

3. Take it one step at a time

Breaking the habit of negative self-talk can be challenging. If practicing self-compassion feels difficult, start small. Find ways to be kind to yourself through self-care activities. Treat yourself to something special, indulge in a relaxing bath, or enjoy a favorite beverage. Self-compassion and self-care go hand in hand, both helping you show kindness towards yourself.

4. Use reminders to stay on track

Sometimes, we're not even aware of how harshly we're treating ourselves. Placing reminders around your home can be a great way to encourage self-compassion. Sticky notes with messages like "Be kind" on your mirror, refrigerator, or even bookmarks can help interrupt negative self-talk and remind you to practice self-compassion.

5. Connect with others who understand

Joining support groups or online communities or reading blogs about living with depression can remind you that you're not alone. It's important to realize that what you're going through is not a failure on your part. By sharing in the journeys of others, you can cultivate compassion for them and recognize that it applies to your own experiences as well.

Practicing the RAIN Techniques

Have you ever heard of the "RAIN" strategy? It's a simple and helpful technique used in mindfulness to navigate your emotions and cope with stressful situations (Verastegui, n.d.).

It's a simple way to practice mindfulness and compassion in these four steps:

1. **R**ecognize: Notice what's happening and acknowledge your feelings.
2. **A**llow: Allow the experience to be there without judgment or resistance.
3. **I**nvestigate: Curiously explore your thoughts and emotions with care.
4. **N**urture: Treat yourself with kindness and self-compassion.

1. You can use RAIN as a meditation practice or apply it whenever you're facing difficult emotions. Take your time and give it a try.

Managing Depression with ACT

Have you heard of acceptance and commitment therapy (ACT)? It's a type of therapy that combines mindfulness and cognitive-behavioral techniques. It has been shown to be really effective in helping people with various health issues (Nash, 2022).

ACT was created by clinical psychologist Steven C. Hayes, who developed it as a way to manage his own panic disorder. He has shared his personal story and how it led to the development of ACT in a TED Talk (TEDx Talks, 2016).

This therapy has proven helpful in managing chronic pain, addictions, anxiety, depression, obsessive-compulsive disorder, and psychosis. There's a lot of scientific evidence supporting its effectiveness.

- ACT focuses on accepting your thoughts and feelings instead of fighting them.
- It helps you to identify your values and set goals that align with what's important to you.
- ACT teaches you to be present in the moment and not get caught up in negative thoughts about the past or worries about the future.
- It encourages you to take committed action toward your goals, even when you're feeling down or unmotivated.
- ACT can be used alongside other treatments for depression, like medication or talk therapy.
- Many people have found ACT helpful in reducing their symptoms of depression and improving their overall wellbeing.

ACT Worksheets for Depression

Worksheet 1: The Power of Acceptance

1. List three things about yourself or your life that you've been struggling to accept.

____

____

____

2. Imagine what your life would look like if you fully accepted those things. How would it feel? How would it change your perspective? Write it down.

____

____

____

3. Write down three actions you can take to start accepting these aspects of your life. Remember that it doesn't mean you have to like everything; it means you're acknowledging and making peace with reality instead.

____

____

____

____

Worksheet 2: Showering Yourself with Self-Compassion

1. Make a list of five things you love about yourself.

____

____

____

2. Write a kind, compassionate letter to yourself, as if you were talking to your best friend. Remind yourself of your strengths, your resilience, and your unique quirks.

____

____

____

Worksheet 3: Defusing the Funk

1. Write down three negative thoughts that often pop up when you're feeling down. Be specific! What's that inner critic whispering in your ear?

____

____

____

2. Imagine those thoughts as characters or objects.

____

____

---

3. Come up with a funny, quirky way to respond to each thought. Remember, we're defusing the funk here! Make those thoughts lose their power with humor.

Worksheet 4: Dancing with Values

1. List five values that are important to you in life. Think about what makes your heart sing, what gets you fired up, and what brings you joy.

---

2. Rate your current level of alignment with each value on a scale of 1 to 10. Be brutally honest with yourself. Where are you slacking? Where are you rocking it?

---

3. Choose one value that you want to focus on right now, and identify one small action you can take today to bring you closer to that value.

____

____

____

Chapter Takeaway

This chapter is sensitive because of the nature of the topic we discussed. I wrote this chapter with special care because I don't want you to join the number of people whose lives have been cut short due to depression.

Depression isn't a life sentence—don't forget that. And it isn't your fault. You can come out of it by practicing any of the techniques that I have highlighted in this chapter, and with the support of a professional therapist if needed.

P.S As you advance through the chapters of this book, your thoughts and reflections may be a guide for many. Your feedback will shape the path and enrich fellow readers' experience.

Before you dive into the next chapter, we invite you to take a few seconds to share your feedback below. **Your review** ignites the conversation and encourages an ongoing narrative to help others.

Thank you for being an active part of this ongoing quest for knowledge.

With gratitude,

Click **HERE** to leave your review! Or Scan the QR code!

PART 3

Working on Your Mental and Physical Health

You can't be happier than your own mind is. What happens when you try to put up a little act to feign happiness when you're hurting within?

Personally, I know that's an extra pound of pain.

Anyway, the emphasis here is that your mind is pivotal to all you'll ever become and experience in your short time on planet Earth. When you've lost the fervor of happiness, but still feign happiness, your efficiency scorecard will betray you. Thus, it's essential to look after the mind.

Ensuring your mental state is healthy is more important than ever, especially during difficult times. A healthy mind can still pivot you out of a bad situation because it'll keep hope alive.

Thus, the last two chapters of this book focus on the wellbeing of your mind and body in reference to how they influence your happiness and attitude toward living.

Do you know you can remain at peace and happy during a chaotic season? You'll find out more in the following pages of this book.

CHAPTER 7

Controlling Your Mind

"Don't be like the people of this world, but let God change the way you think. Then you will know how to do everything that is good and pleasing to him."

—Romans 12:2

Have you heard about the reporter who had a panic attack while doing a live broadcast on national TV?

His name is Dan Harris. He was a young, ambitious reporter who was striving to make a mark in the industry. When Dan was in his twenties, he was really focused on his work, but, as he has since explained while reflecting back on the panic attack, he also had a negative voice inside his head that made him doubt himself.

After reporting on the Iraq War, he started using drugs to help him cope with his depression.

One day in 2004, while getting ready to do a news update on *Good Morning America*, something unexpected happened. As the cameras were rolling and millions of people were watching, Dan suddenly couldn't breathe. His heart was racing, his mouth was dry, and his palms were sweaty. It was a panic attack.

This panic attack was a major turning point for Dan. He decided to quit using drugs and started exploring mindfulness—something he learned about while working for ABC News.

According to Dan, mindfulness is a skill you can keep getting better at. It's all about being present, focusing your attention, and being kind to yourself and others. Dan admits that he isn't perfect and still has moments of being not-so-great, but affirms that practicing mindfulness has made a big difference in his life.

"Hey! I'm happy you found inner peace and all, but put me down!"

Self-Compassion and Your Cognitive Functioning

This book started with a discussion about self-compassion with an emphasis on *self*. But now, let's go a bit deeper by looking at the impact of self-compassion on cognitive function. Although we're moving outside of the self, we're still staying within the confines of the emphasis of this book—the soul (mind).

What is cognitive functioning?

Fisher et al. (2019) explain that cognitive functioning is all about how our minds work and our different mental abilities. The term covers a whole range of things, like learning, thinking, reasoning, remembering, solving problems, making decisions, and paying attention. Basically, it's everything that goes on in our head when we're using our brain to do things. It's how we process information, come up with ideas, remember things from the past, figure out solutions to problems, make choices, and stay focused on what we're doing.

Our cognitive functioning plays a big role in how we learn new things, how we make sense of the world around us, and how we navigate through life. It's like the engine that powers our thinking and helps us make sense of the world.

What will happen to your performance if your cognition fails? A stressed mind cannot perform optimally, and neither can a depressed mind. This is where practicing self-compassion comes in handy.

One factor that can have a positive impact on cognitive function is self-compassion, which, as you know by now, is how we treat ourselves with kindness and understanding, especially during difficult times. Research suggests that self-compassion is linked to better cognitive function, and here are some key points to understand this relationship:

- Self-compassion helps reduce stress and negative emotions, which can improve our ability to think, learn, and remember things.
- By being kind to ourselves, we create a positive internal environment that supports cognitive processes.
- Self-compassion enhances our attention and focus, allowing us to better concentrate on tasks and absorb information.
- It promotes a positive mindset and helps us approach challenges with resilience, leading to more effective problem-solving and decision-making.
- Practicing self-compassion cultivates a healthy and balanced mindset* that supports our cognitive abilities.

*Discover simple tips to develop a Joyful Mindset and unleash your Happy Hormones. Work on Worksheet #2 by downloading the BONUS of this book.

Being Grounded for Mental Clarity

Grounding means tuning in to the present moment and becoming more aware of what's happening around you. It's a way to connect with your surroundings, understand how they fit into the bigger picture of your life, and become more in touch with your own emotions. It's all about being present and aware in the here and now (The Light Program, 2019).

Grounding is a technique that taps into your five senses to help you calm and comfort yourself when you're feeling overwhelmed. Essentially, you can use what you see, touch, hear, smell, and even taste to bring yourself back to the present moment and find a sense of stability. Focusing on your senses will anchor you, allowing you to find a sense of relief during challenging times.

Jacquelyn Van Zile, a licensed professional clinical counselor (LPCC), has recommended the following grounding techniques (General Health Team, 2022):

Mental grounding

Mental grounding techniques are helpful for shifting your thoughts away from negativity and stress. Here are some examples:

- **Categories game:** Think of as many things as possible within a specific category. (You may have played a similar game with friends while growing up.) For instance, name as many mammals as you can think of, or as many countries as you can think of.

- **Describe your surroundings:** Take a moment to look around and describe your environment to yourself. Be as detailed as you can, but stick to the reality of what you see and avoid adding emotions or opinions to your description.

Physical grounding

Physical grounding techniques involve focusing on something you can touch or a sensation. Here are a few examples:

- **The five senses:** Stimulate one of your senses. For example, if you're using the sense of smell, take a whiff of something strong, like peppermint or coffee beans. For the sense of taste, you can take a bite of something with a strong flavor, like a grapefruit or licorice. Whatever you choose, pay attention to the feedback your senses give you.
- **Music:** Pick some neutral music to listen to—it should be something that doesn't bring up strong emotions for you.

Soothing grounding

Soothing grounding techniques are all about finding comfort in the things that you like and that give you a sense of identity. Here are a couple of examples:

- **Your favorite things:** Just like the song from *The Sound of Music*, think about all your favorite things—whether that's your favorite season, song, book, food, etc. Think about all the reasons you like those things.
- **Comforting photos:** Keep photos that soothe you nearby, like a picture from a memorable trip you took, or a photo of yourself with family or a good friend.

It can be helpful to have someone else practice these techniques with you. Why? Believe it or not, just being in someone else's presence and hearing their voice can make a difference in grounding yourself.

The Neuroplastic Effect of Mindfulness

The neuroplastic effect of mindfulness refers to the changes that occur in the brain as a result of practicing mindfulness. Here's what you need to know:

- **Brain plasticity:** The brain has the remarkable ability to change and reorganize itself throughout life. This is known as neuroplasticity. Mindfulness has been found to have a positive impact on brain plasticity.
- **Structural changes:** Research suggests that regular mindfulness practice can lead to structural changes in the brain, particularly in areas associated with attention, emotional regulation, and self-awareness. These

changes can enhance cognitive function and emotional wellbeing.

- **Increased gray matter:** Mindfulness has been linked to an increase in gray matter volume in certain brain regions, such as the prefrontal cortex and the hippocampus. These areas are involved in executive functions, memory, and emotional regulation.
- **Strengthened connections:** Mindfulness practice can strengthen the connections between different regions of the brain, improving communication and integration. This can enhance cognitive abilities, emotional resilience, and overall mental wellbeing.
- **Regulation of stress response:** Mindfulness has been shown to modulate the brain's stress response, reducing activity in the amygdala (the brain's fear center) and increasing activity in the prefrontal cortex (responsible for rational thinking and decision-making). This helps in managing stress and promoting a sense of calm.
- **Long-term benefits:** The neuroplastic effects of mindfulness are not just temporary. Regular and sustained practice can lead to long-term changes in the brain, resulting in improved cognitive functioning, emotional regulation, and overall mental health.

Resilience and Healthy Coping with Self-Compassion

Resilience and healthy coping are essential for navigating life's challenges, and self-compassion plays a crucial role in developing these qualities. Here's how self-compassion can contribute to resilience and healthy coping:

- **Acceptance of imperfections:** Self-compassion involves recognizing and accepting our own imperfections, acknowledging that everyone makes mistakes and faces difficulties. This mindset helps us bounce back from setbacks and view them as opportunities for growth rather than personal failures.
- **Kindness towards oneself:** Self-compassion encourages treating ourselves as we would treat a friend who is going through a tough time. By offering ourselves compassion and support, we develop a nurturing inner voice that helps us cope with stress and adversity.
- **Emotional regulation:** Self-compassion helps us regulate our emotions effectively. Instead of suppressing or ignoring difficult emotions, we acknowledge them with kindness and non-judgment. This allows us to process and manage our emotions in a healthier way, which promotes resilience in the face of challenges.
- **Reduced self-criticism:** Self-compassion helps to counteract self-critical thoughts and self-blame. When

faced with difficulties, we tend to be our own harshest critics. However, self-compassion allows us to respond to setbacks with encouragement and understanding, fostering resilience and motivating us to keep going.

- **Building a support network:** Self-compassion enables us to cultivate healthy relationships and seek support when needed. When we value ourselves and our wellbeing, we are more likely to reach out to others for help and build a supportive network. This social support is crucial for coping with stress and enhancing resilience.
- **Self-care practices:** Self-compassion encourages self-care, which involves prioritizing our physical, emotional, and mental wellbeing. Engaging in activities that promote self-care, such as exercise, relaxation techniques, hobbies, and enjoyable experiences, enhances resilience by providing us with the necessary resources to cope with stress.

Applying Self-Compassion to Challenging Situations

Applying self-compassion to challenging situations can help us navigate difficulties with greater understanding, resilience, and kindness toward ourselves. Here are my recommendations for applying self-compassion in challenging situations:

Recognize common humanity

Remind yourself that everyone faces challenges and struggles at some point. You are not alone in experiencing difficulties. Recognizing our shared humanity helps us feel connected to others and reduces feelings of isolation.

Practice self-kindness

Treat yourself with kindness, care, and understanding, just as you would treat a friend in need. Offer yourself words of comfort and encouragement, acknowledging that it's okay to make mistakes and face obstacles. Be patient and gentle with yourself as you navigate the challenges.

Validate your emotions

Acknowledge and validate your emotions without judgment. It's normal to feel upset, frustrated, or overwhelmed in challenging situations. Instead of suppressing or denying your emotions, allow yourself to fully experience them while offering yourself compassion and understanding.

Reframe negative self-talk

Notice any negative self-talk or self-critical thoughts that arise during challenging situations. Challenge and reframe them by replacing them with kind, supportive, and realistic thoughts.

Don't isolate yourself

Reach out to trusted friends, family, or professionals who can provide support and guidance during challenging times. Sharing your experiences and seeking assistance is an act of self-compassion and shows that you value your wellbeing.

Learn and move on from setbacks

View failures as opportunities for growth and learning. Embrace the lessons that challenging situations offer and see them as stepping stones towards personal development and resilience. Remember that mistakes and difficulties are a normal part of life, and they do not define your worth or capabilities.

Engage in self-care

Prioritize self-care activities that nurture your physical, emotional, and mental wellbeing. Take breaks when needed, engage in activities you enjoy, practice relaxation techniques, exercise, get enough sleep, and eat nourishing foods. Taking care of yourself supports your overall resilience and helps you better cope with challenges.

If you act on each of these recommendations, you will be better able to develop a compassionate, perceptive, and resilient mindset toward yourself—thereby empowering you to face difficulties with greater compassion and navigate them in a healthier and more supportive way.

Mindfulness Exercises for Improving Focus and Clarity

Let's take a look at a few more mindfulness exercises to enhance your focus and clarity.

Slow down and be present

In our busy world, it can be challenging to slow down and truly notice things. Take the time to engage your senses and fully experience your environment. Pay attention to the sounds, sights, smells, and perhaps tastes around you. For example, when you eat your favorite food, savor the moment by smelling, tasting, and enjoying it.

Embrace the now

Make a conscious effort to live in the present moment. Approach each activity with an open, accepting, and attentive mindset. Find joy in the simple pleasures that surround you, whether it's the warmth of sunlight on your skin or the sound of birds chirping.

Practice self-acceptance

Treat yourself with the compassion you give to your close friends. Accept yourself as you are, embracing both your strengths and imperfections. Remember that it's okay to make mistakes and that self-acceptance is an important part of personal growth.

Resilience Worksheet

Section 1: Reflect on Your Past Triumphs

1. Remember That Time You Conquered a Challenge:

Think back to a time when you overcame a difficult situation—maybe getting through a difficult exam, conquering a fear, or overcoming a personal setback. Detail your experience, including how you felt, what you did, and how it affected your personal development. Relive your accomplishment to bolster your confidence.

____

____

____

____

____

2. Your Resilience Recipe:

Identify the traits and strategies that helped you get through the challenge. Was it your perseverance, your upbeat outlook, the encouragement of your loved ones, or a special strategy? List the key ingredients in your recipe for resilience. They will serve as reminders of what works best for you when times are tough.

____

____

Section 2: Supercharging Your Resilience

3. Embrace the Power of Gratitude:

Make a list of at least five items in your life for which you are grateful at the moment. They could be significant or insignificant, from loved ones to small pleasures that make you happy. Gratitude practice aids in shifting your focus to the positive aspects of your life and boosts resilience.

4. Your Support Squad:

As a superhero, no one takes on life alone! Find out who in your life is always there for you and offers unflinching support. It may be close relatives, close friends, mentors, or even online communities. List their names and the ways they have previously assisted you. In trying times, reaching out to your support network is a sign of strength, not weakness.

____

____

____

____

____

5. Flex Your Resilience Muscles:

Resilience is like a muscle that needs regular exercise to grow stronger. Identify an area in your life where you can challenge yourself and step out of your comfort zone. It could be trying a new hobby, setting a fitness goal, or learning a new skill. Write down your chosen challenge and outline the steps you'll take to achieve it. Remember, even small steps count!

____

____

____

____

____

Section 3: Building Resilience in Daily Life

6. Taming the Inner Critic:

Everybody has that inner voice that likes to criticize them. Make a note of the phrases you use the most often to criticize yourself. Now, respond to those statements with positive, empowering affirmations. If your inner critic tells you, "You're not good enough," for instance, respond, "I am capable of anything I set my mind to!" Daily repetition of these affirmations will retrain your brain to be resilient.

____

____

____

____

____

7. The Power of Play:

Being robust does not necessitate being solemn all of the time! Find activities that you enjoy and that make you feel carefree. It could be as simple as playing with your pet, singing in the shower, dancing, or going on a walk. Make a list of fun things to do and commit to doing at least one of them every day. Remember that having fun and laughing are essential for building resilience.

____

____

____

____

____

8. Learning from Setbacks:

It is more important to bounce back stronger from setbacks than to avoid them. Write down the lessons you learned from a recent setback or failure. How can you use those lessons to advance your development?

____

____

____

____

____

Section 4: Cultivating Resilience in Relationships

9. Building Empathy Bridges:

Being resilient involves more than just bouncing back; it also involves supporting and understanding others. To develop empathy, try to imagine yourself in another person's position. List three ways you might show support and empathy for a person in your life who is struggling. It might be done by listening attentively, offering a helping hand, or just by being present.

____

____

____

Section 5: Your Resilient Future

10. Vision of Resilience:

Think of your future self as a tough superhero. Give specific examples of how this version of yourself solves issues, keeps a positive outlook, and motivates others. Make a list of the traits, actions, and mindset that your resilient future self will possess. This vision will act as a source of inspiration and optimism for daily resilience building.

---

11. Your Resilience Toolkit:

Create a list of resources, strategies, and activities that you can turn to when you need an extra boost of resilience. It could include inspirational books, uplifting podcasts, meditation exercises, or motivational quotes. Refer back to this toolkit whenever you need a reminder of the tools at your disposal to overcome any obstacle.

____

____

____

____

____

Chapter Takeaway

A few things I'd like you to remember in this chapter include:

- Your mind is pivotal to everything you'll ever become. Therefore, guide and care for your mind well.
- Self-compassion is a practice that can optimize your cognition. It can enhance your performance even when you're performing below par.
- Self-compassion can also help you scale mountains and go through the tempestuous moments of life without drowning.
- The practice of self-compassion can build resilience in you to survive difficult seasons of life.

Self-compassion takes time and patience. Therefore, don't rush through the steps in an attempt to get instant results. This is a lifelong practice that promises to yield life-transforming results.

CHAPTER 8

Self-Care for Happiness

"Are you tired? Worn out? Burned out...? Come to me. Get away with me and you'll recover your life. I'll show you how to take a real rest... Learn the unforced rhythms of grace. I won't lay anything heavy or ill-fitting on you. Keep company with me and you'll learn to live freely and lightly."

—Matthew 11:28-30

While I was putting this book together, the story of a particular young man caught my attention. This young man was multi-talented; he led a group of young religious people and was also a professional sign language interpreter, a wedding photographer, a radio host, a husband, and a father. Wow!

As an interpreter, he attended all of his students' after-school activities. On top of that, he had a radio show on Tuesday and Friday nights, church functions on Wednesday nights and on the weekend, and Sundays were filled with photographing weddings or youth group activities. His days were long, and he barely had any time to himself.

In his righteous mind, he believed that his constant busyness was making his wife proud. After all, he was doing so much for the church! However, in his lack of personal boundaries, he was unintentionally building walls between himself and the people who loved him the most. He didn't know it was okay, and even necessary, to say "no" to others, to take a day off, to switch off his phone, and to spend quality time with those who longed for his affection and attention.

As his personal relationships crumbled, he began to feel trapped and lost, drowning in shame and panic attacks that seemed to be happening more and more frequently. Eventually, the stress became too much for him to bear, and he reached a point of desperation, feeling utterly defeated.

But amidst the darkness, he found a glimmer of hope. He realized that he needed to prioritize his own wellbeing and recovery. He embarked on a journey of self-care, learning invaluable tips and tricks along the way to nurture his mental and emotional health. That's when he discovered the importance of self-care and the power it holds in maintaining a balanced and fulfilling life.

The truth remains: nothing is worth giving up your self-care for. When you cease to exist, those things will continue to exist. Someone else will continue where you left off. So why the stress?

Finding Happiness Through a Self-Care Routine

Self-care is all about consciously and intentionally taking care of our mental, physical, and emotional wellbeing. It involves engaging in activities that nourish and support our overall health (Adam, 2023). I'd like to emphasize that taking care of yourself is not selfish but is, in fact, essential for cultivating deeper connections with yourself and those around you.

You can try these self-care routines:

1. **Daily reflection:** Take a few moments each day for quiet reflection or meditation. This can help calm your mind and bring a sense of inner peace.
2. **Pursuing joy:** Engage in activities that bring you joy and happiness. It could be reading your favorite books, baking, listening to music, or engaging in any hobby that uplifts your spirits.
3. **Exercise:** Regular physical activity is important for your overall health. Find an exercise routine that you enjoy, whether it's going for a walk, dancing, or playing a sport.
4. **Healthy eating:** Pay attention to your diet and nourish your body with nutritious foods. Eating a balanced diet can have a positive impact on your energy levels and overall wellbeing.

5. **Sufficient sleep:** Make sure you get enough restful sleep each night. Establish a bedtime routine that promotes relaxation and creates a conducive environment for quality sleep.
6. **Setting boundaries:** Learn to set boundaries with others. It's okay to say "no" when you need time for yourself or when something doesn't align with your wellbeing.

"Are you sure you don't want to use it for yourself?"

The Role of Self-Care in Overall Wellbeing

Sometimes, when things get tough, we tend to forget about taking care of ourselves. We may prioritize work, money, or dealing with difficult situations. But it's important to remember that self-care should be a priority, especially during challenging times (Glowiak, 2022). It shouldn't be an afterthought, but rather, something we keep in mind every day. When we take care of ourselves, it can make a big difference in how we feel and how we handle tough situations. It's like giving ourselves a boost to stay strong and resilient.

According to Dr. Kaylee Crockett, a clinical psychologist who works in the UAB Department of Family and Community Medicine (cited by Jones, 2022), self-care can mean different things to different people. It could be making sure you eat nutritious meals and get enough sleep. It could be finding activities that bring you joy and help you relax, like reading, painting, or playing a sport. It could also mean taking breaks when you need them, setting boundaries with others, and asking for help when you need it.

Regardless of what self-care means to you, it prods you toward just one goal: your happiness and wellbeing.

What role does self-care play in your wellbeing?

Improved physical health

Self-care involves prioritizing your physical wellbeing. By taking care of your body through activities like regular exercise, proper sleep, and practicing good hygiene, you can enhance your overall physical health.

Reduced stress and anxiety

Engaging in relaxation techniques, such as taking a warm bath or listening to music, is an important aspect of self-care. These activities help reduce stress and anxiety, promoting a more positive mood.

Boosted self-esteem

Taking time to relax and care for yourself can have a positive impact on how you view yourself. Treating yourself with kindness and practicing self-care can improve your self-esteem, making you more resilient in the face of setbacks and more likely to achieve personal goals (Breines & Chen, 2012).

Protection of mental health

Prioritizing self-care can help manage and prevent the worsening of mental health issues. While self-care is not a substitute for professional help, it plays a crucial role in supporting your mental wellbeing. If you are experiencing mental health challenges, it's important to reach out to a professional for assistance.

Improved relationships

When you prioritize self-care and focus on your own happiness and health, it positively impacts your relationships with others. By taking care of yourself, you have more to give to your loved ones, fostering healthier and more fulfilling connections.

Self-Care, Self-Love, and Self-Compassion

These three are essential components of our wellbeing and how we relate to ourselves. They form the foundation of a healthy and fulfilling life.

When we practice **self-love**, we embrace ourselves with kindness, recognizing our worth and inherent value and accepting ourselves for who we are.

Self-care, as we have just discussed, is the intentional act of tending to our physical, mental, and emotional needs. It involves listening to our bodies, nurturing our minds, and engaging in activities that bring us joy and relaxation. By prioritizing self-care, we create space for rejuvenation and renewal, allowing us to show up fully in our lives and relationships.

Self-compassion goes hand in hand with self-love and self-care. As we explored in a previous chapter, it is about being gentle with ourselves when we face challenges or make mistakes. Instead of harsh self-judgment, we offer ourselves understanding, forgiveness, and encouragement. Self-compassion allows us to embrace our imperfections, knowing that they are a natural part of being human.

Together, self-love, self-care, and self-compassion form a powerful trio that nurtures our wellbeing. By cultivating these practices, we honor ourselves, recognize our needs, and create a solid foundation for a life filled with happiness, resilience, and meaningful connections.

Although these three work together and may appear similar on the surface, there are also some subtle differences between them (Gurwitz, 2019). Let's examine them together, shall we?

Self-love:

- Focuses on cultivating a positive and unconditional regard for oneself.
- Involves developing a deep sense of self-worth and self-acceptance.
- Involves treating oneself with kindness, respect, and empathy.

Self-care:

- Refers to the intentional actions taken to meet one's physical, mental, and emotional needs.
- Includes engaging in activities that promote wellbeing, such as exercise, healthy eating, restful sleep, and practicing stress-reduction techniques.
- Involves setting boundaries, saying no when necessary, and prioritizing self-nurturing activities.

Self-compassion:

- Involves being kind, understanding, and forgiving toward oneself during times of difficulty, failure, or suffering.
- Requires acknowledging and validating one's own emotions and experiences without judgment.
- Involves treating oneself with the same compassion and care one would extend to a close friend or loved one.

The Seven Pillars of Self-Care

To maintain a well-rounded self-care routine, it's important to incorporate practices that align with the seven pillars of self-care: mental, emotional, physical, environmental, spiritual, recreational, and social. By engaging in activities from each pillar, you can better nurture your overall wellbeing. Here's a breakdown of each pillar with examples of how to practice them:

1. Mental self-care:

- Engage in stimulating activities like reading, doing puzzles, or learning something new.
- Take time to meditate to calm your mind and improve focus. In Joshua 1:8 and Psalms 1:1-3, God says you will have success in life when you meditate on His Word daily.

- Set goals and challenge yourself intellectually.

2. Emotional self-care:

- Express your feelings through journaling or creative outlets like art or music.
- Seek therapy or counseling to process emotions and gain emotional support.
- Engage in activities that bring you joy and make you feel emotionally fulfilled.

3. Physical self-care:

- Prioritize regular exercise or physical activities that you enjoy.
- Get enough restful sleep to recharge your body.
- Maintain a balanced and nutritious diet for optimal physical health.

4. Environmental self-care:

- Create a clean, organized, and clutter-free living space.
- Spend time in nature, go for walks, or practice gardening.
- Surround yourself with positive and uplifting environments and people.

5. Spiritual self-care:

- Engage in activities that align with your beliefs and values.
- Practice meditation, prayer, or mindfulness to connect with your inner self.
- Spend time in reflection and gratitude, or engage in acts of kindness and compassion.

6. Recreational self-care:

- Engage in hobbies or activities that bring you joy and relaxation.
- Take breaks and enjoy leisure time to recharge and rejuvenate.
- Plan outings, adventures, or trips to explore new experiences.

7. Social self-care:

- Cultivate and maintain healthy relationships with family and friends.
- Seek social support when needed and engage in meaningful connections.
- Participate in social activities, or join clubs or organizations.

Self-Care Practices for Happiness

I've mentioned something similar to this before, but here I'll share some more detailed practices recommended by Dr. Crockett (cited by Jones, 2022):

Maintain a balanced diet

Consume a variety of fruits, vegetables, seafood, and nuts to boost energy levels and enhance focus throughout the day.

Stay hydrated

Drink at least 60 ounces of water daily (more during the hotter months!).

Engage in physical activity

Aim for at least 30 minutes of exercise (e.g., walking) each day, which not only improves mood but also enhances overall health. Remember, even small bursts of movement can make a difference.

Schedule relaxation time

Dedicate a part of your day to activities that reduce stress, such as meditation, deep breathing exercises, listening to music, journaling, or exploring new hobbies. Hobbies can keep the mind engaged and provide opportunities to learn new skills.

Prioritize sleep

Get seven to nine hours of quality sleep each night. Avoid using electronic devices before bedtime, as the blue light can disrupt sleep. Instead, opt for uplifting books or inspiring podcasts.

Cultivate meaningful relationships

Build strong connections with supportive family members and friends. Consider participating in activities that allow you to meet new people, such as classes or support groups. Reach out to loved ones who can offer emotional support and practical assistance.

Are you ready to enjoy even more self-care practices?

I've curated lots of them here for you. Try them at your leisure.

- Take a relaxing bath
- Create something—a painting, a poem, or anything that sparks your creativity
- Spend time in nature, go for a walk in the park, or explore hiking trails
- Enjoy some laughter—watch a comedy show or spend time with funny friends
- Write your future self a letter expressing your hopes and dreams
- Take a day trip to a new place and explore

- Treat yourself to a spa day or indulge in a massage or facial
- Wake up 15 minutes early and savor your morning routine
- Spend quality time with a pet, playing and bonding with them
- Reflect on your accomplishments and celebrate your achievements
- Cook your favorite meal and savor each bite
- Take a break from technology, disconnect, and focus on mindfulness
- Dance to your favorite music and let yourself go
- Go over your finances and create a budget that aligns with your goals
- Volunteer and give back to your community
- Write self-love affirmations and repeat them daily
- Plan a trip, even if it's just a local exploration
- Enjoy your tea or coffee in a cozy spot, savoring the moment
- Try a new hobby or learn something new, expanding your horizons
- Take a nap and prioritize rest and relaxation
- Spend time with friends, family, or colleagues you haven't talked to in a while

- Plant something and nurture it as it grows
- Create a self-care kit with comforting items and activities
- Watch the sunrise or sunset, appreciating the beauty of nature
- Practice gratitude by making a list of things you're thankful for
- Read a good book and immerse yourself in a different world
- Clean up your space and create a clutter-free environment
- Have a spa day at home—pamper yourself with a facial, manicure, or bubble bath
- Buy yourself new sheets or pillows for a cozy and comfortable sleep
- Contribute to a cause you care about
- Write out your five-year plan, setting goals and aspirations
- Take a relaxing shower and enjoy the warm water on your skin
- Enjoy a movie marathon, binge-watching your favorite films or TV series
- Fix something that's broken, whether it's a household item or a personal project

- Be a child again and engage in playful activities or visit an amusement park
- Make a gratitude jar and fill it with notes of appreciation
- Take a self-care day and prioritize your wellbeing above all else
- Explore your creativity by decorating your home with items that bring you joy
- Write down your thoughts and feelings to process and reflect
- Make a positive impact
- Smile at yourself in the mirror, embracing self-love and acceptance
- Engage in recreational activities that bring you joy and relaxation
- Practice deep breathing exercises or meditation to calm your mind and reduce stress
- Engage in mindful eating by consuming a balanced diet and savoring each bite
- Engage in regular physical activity to improve energy levels and overall health
- Engage in social activities and build strong relationships with supportive individuals

- Indulge in hobbies that bring you joy and help you learn new skills
- Write your first entry in a journal and begin the journey of self-reflection
- Go through old photos and reminisce about happy memories
- Enjoy a soothing music playlist that helps you relax and unwind
- Take time to plan and organize your tasks to reduce stress and increase productivity
- Fix or replace items that are worn out or no longer serving their purpose
- Take a moment to express gratitude to someone who has made a positive impact on your life
- Take care of your physical health by scheduling regular checkups and medical appointments

Integrating the Self-Compassionate Lifestyle

As this book draws to a close, it's important for you to know that integrating self-compassion into your life requires honesty and a commitment to seeking the truth. By uprooting misbeliefs and replacing them with self-acceptance and understanding, you can develop self-compassion and transform various aspects of your life.

Implement these three things to integrate self-compassion into your daily life.

1. Cultivate awareness of your internal dialogue

- Take time to listen to your silent self-talk and identify any self-critical or negative thoughts.
- Notice patterns of self-judgment and self-criticism, such as feeling like a failure or believing you are unlovable or unworthy.
- Be mindful of the triggers that evoke these self-critical thoughts and the emotions associated with them.

2. Analyze and challenge your thoughts

- Analyze your thoughts and beliefs, looking for irrational or unhelpful patterns.
- Rate the strength of your belief in the self-critical thoughts on a scale of 0 to 100%.
- Identify the tone of voice used in your self-talk and recognize the impact it has on your emotions.
- Reflect on the triggers that activate self-critical thoughts and examine their validity.

3. Reconstruct your thinking with compassion

- Replace distorted self-beliefs with more realistic and compassionate statements.

- Use a softer and more understanding tone of voice when addressing yourself.
- Imagine how you would offer support and guidance to a friend facing a similar situation.
- Explore alternative perspectives that are kinder, more helpful, and aligned with reality.
- Develop coping strategies and self-care practices to nurture yourself in challenging moments.
- Embrace a compassionate and empowering conclusion that counteracts self-criticism.
- Reassess the strength of your belief in the self-critical thoughts and the intensity of the associated emotions.

Practicing Self-Care Worksheets

Worksheet 1: Your Self-Care Bucket List

1. For a moment, visualize your ideal self-care activities. What practices or activities make you happy, content, and fulfilled?

Make a list of at least five ideas for activities.

____

____

____

2. Select a task from your list that you can complete today or this coming week.

Be practical and pick an activity that you can fit into your schedule.

____

____

____

3. Choose a time and date for the activity you want to do.

Put the time in your calendar and make it a priority.

____

____

____

---

4. Imagine yourself engaging in this activity; consider how it will impact you; consider the benefits it will provide for your overall wellbeing.

Worksheet 2: Embracing Daily Self-Care Rituals

1. Consider your existing daily routine. Are there any opportunities for self-care that you could be missing?

- Look at all times of day (morning, afternoon, and evening).

2. List at least three self-care practices or rituals you can incorporate into your daily schedule.

- It may be as simple as having a cup of tea or taking a stroll through the forest.

---

3. Establish a routine for your new self-care practices.

Set aside specific times of the day and stick to them for each activity.

Date/time	Sunday	Monday	Tuesday	Wednesday	Thursday	Friday	Saturday
Morning	(Self-care activity)						
Afternoon							
Evening							

4. Create a self-care journal to document your progress and the effects of each action. Use it to serve as a reminder of the positive effects self-care can have on your life.

Date	Self-care activity	How it made you feel

Great job finishing the worksheets on self-care! Remember that self-care is a process and not a one-time thing. Keep shining, and enjoy your self-care journey.

Chapter Takeaway

The emphasis of this chapter has been on the application of self-care practices for your wellbeing. To practice self-care, you must take a balanced approach that includes the seven aspects of your being. You can't take care of just one part of yourself and leave the others out.

Remember, you don't need a special, huge block of time to take care of yourself. You just need to readjust your schedule and practice the recommendations in this chapter. You can even create your own self-care practices. The goal is to ensure you're living a happy life.

Conclusion

Throughout this book, we have explored various aspects of happiness, self-compassion, emotional health, and self-care. By delving into the chapters and reflecting on the valuable insights within them, you have taken significant steps toward a happier and more fulfilling life.

In Part 1, we learned that self-compassion is a key ingredient in the recipe for happiness. Being kind to yourself and treating yourself with understanding and acceptance is the foundation of self-compassion.

Remember, it's okay to be gentle with yourself and embrace your imperfections. By practicing self-compassion, you can foster a positive relationship with yourself, leading to greater happiness.

Moving on to Part 2, we explored themes related to your emotional health. The dominant practice for having emotional stability discussed in this part was mindfulness. Mindful self-compassion emerged as a powerful tool to navigate the ups and downs of life. By practicing mindfulness and extending compassion toward yourself, you can cultivate emotional resilience and find peace within.

Additionally, we discovered the vital connection between self-esteem and happiness, understanding that building a healthy sense of self-esteem is crucial for our overall wellbeing.

Part 3 shed light on the significance of nurturing both your mental and physical health. Strengthening your mind through self-compassion, mindfulness, and a positive mindset can empower you to thrive in difficult times.

Self-care, as highlighted in Chapter 8, plays a pivotal role in your happiness journey. Taking time to care for yourself and engaging in activities that bring joy and relaxation is a powerful way to enhance your wellbeing.

Remember, happiness is a lifelong journey that requires dedication and effort. It's normal to experience setbacks and face challenges along the way. The key is to approach these obstacles with resilience, compassion, and mindfulness, grounded in the moment.

Keep in mind also that happiness is not about being in a constant state of bliss. It is an attitude. It's about finding contentment and meaning in the journey itself.

As you conclude this book, I encourage you to continue exploring, learning, and practicing the principles shared here. Embrace self-compassion, nurture your emotional wellbeing, and prioritize self-care. Cultivate a positive mindset and surround yourself with supportive relationships.

Happiness is a personal experience, and each individual's path may look different.

Final Note

God created humans to live a long, fulfilling, happy life. He provided everything we'd ever need to live a happy life. He created an enabling environment for us as well. All we had to do was take care of our habitat.

Sounds great, doesn't it?

But humans messed up that opportunity. The world is full of chaos today because the first humans messed up a golden opportunity to live happily forever.

But it's not fair to just keep blaming those first humans. We have the opportunity to make our choices today and choose how we live. We can rewrite our destiny and decide we want to live happily from now on.

First, I'm extending an invitation to you to embrace a life of unending rest and happiness. Your first and most important decision is to accept this invitation. You have to let go of the burdens of sorrow, pain, and hurt (Matthew 11:28-30).

Then, decide to trust God, the Potter, to make all things new in your life (Jeremiah 18:1-6; Isaiah 26:3; Isaiah 43:18-19).

That's how to enjoy eternal rest and peace that no human mind can comprehend.

I wish you a life filled with genuine happiness, resilience, and a deep sense of fulfillment. Embrace the lessons you've learned and carry them forward on your journey toward lasting happiness. Within you, you can find the will to create a life that brings you joy and purpose.

Now, go out there and live your happiest life!

I'd like to share in your happiness. Just write to me and give me feedback on how your happiness journey has been. Or better still, leave a public review on Amazon. Thank you so much.

Thank You

Dear reader,

Your Feedback Matters!

THANK YOU SO MUCH for getting this book and making it to the end.

We'd love to hear you as you've finished with the last chapter of the Happiness Returns book. Your words have the power to shape the reading perspective of fellow readers. Could you please, write your insights and favorite takeaways from this book? And tell others how this book has influenced you.

Leaving a review can take just a few seconds. But these words can have a lasting influence on others.

Writing a feedback can be fast. But this can have an amplified impact on many readers.

I would love to hear from you.

Your review is precious!

Thank you!

Warmest regards,

Robert

>> Leave a review on Amazon US << 

>> Leave a review on Amazon UK << 

References

A Little Dose of Happy (2023). *52 surprisingly simple self-care ideas to boost happiness!* A Little Dose of Happy. Retrieved from https://aldohappy.com/self-care-ideas

Academy of Ideas (2015). *The ideas of Socrates.* Academy of Ideas. Retrieved from https://academyofideas.com/2015/03/the-ideas-of-socrates-transcript/

Ackerman, C. E. (2017). *Mindfulness-based stress reduction: The ultimate MBSR guide.* PositivePsychology.com. Retrieved from https://positivepsychology.com/mindfulness-based-stress-reduction-mbsr/

Ackerman, C. E. (2019). *What is happiness and why is it important? (+ definition).* PositivePsychology.com. Retrieved from https://positivepsychology.com/what-is-happiness/

Admin. (2022). *Aristotle's concept of the self.* Philo-Notes. Retrieved from https://philonotes.com/2022/05/aristotles-concept-of-the-self

Alavi, K. (2021). The role of social safeness and self-compassion in mental health problems: A model based on gilbert theory of emotion regulation systems. *Practice in Clinical Psychology, 9*(3), 237–246. https://doi.org/10.32598/jpcp.9.3.768.1

Austin, S. (2017). *3 examples of self-care in the bible.* HuffPost. Retrieved from https://www.huffpost.com/entry/3-examples-of-selfcare-in_b_13073572

Brach, T. (2023). *RAIN: A practice of radical compassion.* Tara Brach. Retrieved from https://www.tarabrach.com/rain/

Breines, J. G., & Chen, S. (2012). Self-compassion increases self-improvement motivation. *Personality and Social Psychology Bulletin, 38*(9), 1133–1143. https://doi.org/10.1177/0146167212445599

Burkett, M. (n.d.). *The seven pillars of self-care.* University of Kansas Recreation Services. Retrieved from https://recreation.ku.edu/seven-pillars-self-care

Carers Trust (n.d.). *Taking care of yourself.* Carers.org. Retrieved from https://carers.org/taking-care-of-yourself/taking-care-of-yourself

Cascio, C. N., O'Donnell, M. B., Tinney, F. J., Lieberman, M. D., Taylor, S. E., Strecher, V. J., & Falk, E. B. (2015). Self-affirmation activates brain systems associated with self-related processing and reward and is reinforced by future orientation. *Social Cognitive and Affective Neuroscience, 11*(4), 621–629. https://doi.org/10.1093/scan/nsv136

Chaieb, L., Hoppe, C., & Fell, J. (2022). Mind wandering and depression: A status report. *Neuroscience & Biobehavioral Reviews, 133*, 104505. https://doi.org/10.1016/j.neubiorev.2021.12.028

Cherry, K. (2022a). *How do psychologists define happiness?* Verywell Mind. Retrieved from https://www.verywellmind.com/what-is-happiness-4869755

Cherry, K. (2022b). *What are the signs of healthy or low self-esteem?* Verywell Mind. Retrieved from https://www.verywellmind.com/what-is-self-esteem-2795868

Cleveland Clinic (2020). *6 ways to build a healthy self-image.* Cleveland Clinic Health Essentials. Retrieved from https://health.clevelandclinic.org/ways-to-build-a-healthy-self-image/

Coates, D. (2022). *A tragic true story about low self-esteem.* Dr. Denny Coates. Retrieved from https://drdennycoates.com/a-tragic-true-story-about-low-self-esteem/

Cole, P. M., Michel, M. K., & Teti, L. O. D. (1994). The development of emotion regulation and dysregulation: A clinical perspective. *Monographs of the Society for Research in Child Development, 59*(2-3), 73–102.

Davidson, R. J., & Begley, S. (2012). *The emotional life of your brain: How its unique patterns affect the way you think, feel, and live—and how you can change them.* London: Penguin.

Education, A. D., & Bergeman, C. S. (2004). The complexity of emotions in later life. *The Journals of Gerontology: Series B, 59*(3), 117–122. https://doi.org/10.1093/geronb/59.3.p117

Fahkry, T. (2017). *Why self-compassion and self-acceptance are the foundations for optimal living.* Medium. Retrieved from https://medium.com/the-mission/why-self-compassion-and-self-acceptance-are-the-foundations-to-optimal-living-7a7df24ffd3e

Fisher, G. G., Chacon, M., & Chaffee, D. S. (2019). Chapter 2 – Theories of cognitive aging and work. *Work Across the Lifespan*, 17–45. https://doi.org/10.1016/b978-0-12-812756-8.00002-5

Foster, C. (2013). *Happiness – an emotion, a mood, a goal or a way of life?* Clare Rose Foster. Retrieved from https://www.clarerosefoster.co.uk/2013/04/happiness-an-emotion-a-mood-a-goal-or-a-way-of-life/

Frank Porter Graham Program on Mindfulness & Self-Compassion (2023). *The three components of self-compassion.* The University of North Carolina at Chapel Hill. Retrieved from https://selfcompassion.web.unc.edu/what-is-self-compassion/the-three-components-of-self-compassion/

Geller, J., Samson, L., Maiolino, N., Iyar, M. M., Kelly, A. C., & Srikameswaran, S. (2022). Self-compassion and its barriers: predicting outcomes from inpatient and residential eating disorders treatment. *Journal of Eating Disorders, 10*(1). https://doi.org/10.1186/s40337-022-00640-8

General Health Team (2022). *What is grounding and how can it improve your mental health?* (n.d.). ProMedica News Network. Retrieved from https://promedicanewsnetwork.org/general-health/what-is-grounding-and-how-can-it-improve-your-mental-health/

Gilbert, P., McEwan, K., Matos, M., & Rivis, A. (2011). Fears of compassion: Development of three self-report measures. *Psychology and Psychotherapy: Theory, Research and Practice, 84*(3), 239–255. https://doi.org/10.1348/147608310x526511

Gilbertson, T. (2010). Self-esteem vs. self-criticism. GoodTherapy. Retrieved from https://www.goodtherapy.org/blog/self-esteem-vs-self-criticism/

Gillette, H. (2021). *7 ways to practice self-compassion when you have depression*. Psych Central. Retrieved from https://psychcentral.com/depression/ways-to-practice-self-compassion-when-you-have-depression

Glowiak, M. (2020). *Why is self-care important?* Southern New Hampshire University. Retrieved from https://www.snhu.edu/about-us/newsroom/health/what-is-self-care

GoodTherapy (2018). *Compassion-focused therapy.* GoodTherapy. Retrieved from https://www.goodtherapy.org/learn-about-therapy/types/compassion-focused-therapy

Graham, B. (1955). *How you can find true happiness.* New Life Newspaper. Retrieved from https://www.newlifepublishing.co.uk/articles/how-you-can-find-true-happiness/

Gries, A. (2023). *Finding true happiness through self-awareness and self-care.* Awakenings Health. Retrieved from https://awakeningshealth.com/2023/02/06/finding-true-happiness-through-self-awareness-and-self-care/

Gross, J. J. (1998). The emerging field of emotion regulation: An integrative review. *Review of General Psychology, 2*(3), 271–299. https://doi.org/10.1037/1089-2680.2.3.271

Gupta, S. (2023). *How to improve your self-worth and why it's important.* Verywell Mind. Retrieved from https://www.verywellmind.com/what-is-self-worth-6543764

Gurwitz, K. (2019). *How self-love, self-care and self-compassion are different (and also irrelevant)*. Thrive Global. Retrieved from https://community.thriveglobal.com/how-self-love-self-care-and-self-compassion-are-different-and-also-irrelevant/

Hannan, J. (2020). The power of self-acceptance and self-compassion. Morency Therapy. Retrieved from https://www.morency.co.uk/the-power-of-self-acceptance-and-self-compassion/

Hanson, R. (2013). *Hardwiring happiness: The new brain science of contentment, calm, and confidence*. New York: Harmony.

Hill, A. (2021). *Identifying "emotional complexity" in loved ones*. News Center Maine. Retrieved from https://www.newscentermaine.com/article/news/local/207/207-interview/identifying-emotional-complexity-in-loved-ones-mood-change-psychology/97-6b802c6f-bb96-4564-a722-6848e262ade4

Hoshaw, C. (2022). *What is mindfulness? A simple practice for greater wellbeing*. Healthline. Retrieved from https://www.healthline.com/health/mind-body/what-is-mindfulness

Huijer, H. (2020). *Inspiring stories on finding true happiness (by Syrian refugees)*. Tracking Happiness. Retrieved from https://www.trackinghappiness.com/inspiring-stories-finding-happiness-syrian-refugees/

Jones, A. (2022). *Self-care: What is it? Why is it so important for your health?* University of Alabama at Birmingham | UAB News. Retrieved from https://www.uab.edu/news/youcanuse/item/13176-self-care-what-is-it-why-is-it-so-important-for-your-health

Kable, R. (2016). *10 mindful & powerful tips to boost your confidence*. Rachael Kable. Retrieved from https://www.rachaelkable.com/blog/mindful-and-powerful-confidence-tips

Kashyap, R. (2022). *Spice of life | Happiness is matter of choice, a state of mind.* Hindustan Times. Retrieved from https://www.hindustantimes.com/cities/chandigarh-news/spice-of-life-happiness-is-matter-of-choice-a-state-of-mind-101666914721125.html

Killingsworth, M. A., & Gilbert, D. T. (2010). A wandering mind is an unhappy mind. *Science, 330*(6006), 932. https://doi.org/10.1126/science.1192439

Lebow, H. I., & Casabianca, S. S. (2022). *Do you know how to manage your emotions and why it matters?* Psych Central. Retrieved from https://psychcentral.com/health/emotional-regulation

Lechner, T. (2019). *5 steps to detaching for a happier life.* Chopra. Retrieved from https://chopra.com/articles/5-steps-to-detaching-for-a-happier-life

Lee, D. A. (2005). The perfect nurturer: A model to develop a compassionate mind within the context of cognitive therapy. In P. Gilbert (Ed.), *Compassion: Conceptualisations, research and use in psychotherapy*, 326–351. Abingdon, UK: Routledge.

Light Program, The. (2019). *Using grounding coping skills to manage your mental health symptoms.* The Light Program. Retrieved from https://thelightprogram.pyramidhealthcarepa.com/grounding-techniques/

MacBeth, A., & Gumley, A. (2012). Exploring compassion: A meta-analysis of the association between self-compassion and psychopathology. *Clinical Psychology Review, 32*(6), 545–552. https://doi.org/10.1016/j.cpr.2012.06.003

Mayo Clinic Staff (2022). *How to stop negative self-talk.* Mayo Clinic. Retrieved from https://www.mayoclinic.org/healthy-lifestyle/stress-management/in-depth/positive-thinking/art-20043950

Mead, E. (2019). *What is mindful self-compassion? (Incl. exercises + PDF).* PositivePsychology.com. Retrieved from https://positivepsychology.com/mindful-self-compassion/

Merriam-Webster. (2023). *Self.* Merriam-Webster. Retrieved from https://www.merriam-webster.com/dictionary/self

Miller, K. (2020). *What is emotional health? (+ 11 activities & examples).* PositivePsychology.com. Retrieved from https://positivepsychology.com/emotional-health-activities/

Moore, C. (2019). *How to practice self-compassion: 8 techniques and tips.* PositivePsychology.com. Retrieved from https://positivepsychology.com/how-to-practice-self-compassion/

Nasir, I. (2019). *You are your own worst critic.* Medium. Retrieved from https://medium.com/swlh/you-are-your-own-worst-critic-fa984ff86dda

Nash, J. (2022). *ACT therapy techniques: 14+ interventions for your sessions.* PositivePsychology.com. Retrieved from https://positivepsychology.com/act-techniques/

Neff, K. (2019) *Tips for practice.* Self-Compassion.org. Retrieved from https://self-compassion.org/tips-for-practice/

Neff, K. (2020). *5 myths of self compassion.* Mindful Schools. Retrieved from https://www.mindfulschools.org/personal-practice/5-myths-of-self-compassion/

Nesse, R. M. (2000). Is depression an adaptation? *Archives of General Psychiatry, 57*(1), 14–20. https://doi.org/10.1001/archpsyc.57.1.14

Olliver, J. (2023). *The emotional reset technique: Master your emotions.* Psychosexual Alignment. Retrieved from https://www.endtheproblem.com/emotional-reset-technique-jacqui-olliver/

Purohit, V. (2022). *What is true happiness?* Times of India. Retrieved from https://timesofindia.indiatimes.com/readersblog/thetinybook/what-is-true-happiness-44628/

Recovery Editorial Staff (2018). *7 ways to combat negative self-talk.* Footprints to Recovery. Retrieved from https://footprintstorecovery.com/blog/combat-negative-self-talk/

Sakhaee, E. (2019). *Self acceptance and self compassion.* educationdIn. Retrieved from https://www.linkedin.com/pulse/self-acceptance-compassion-ehssan-sakhaee-phd

Scott, E. (2022a). *Can mindfulness relieve more than stress?* Verywell Mind. Retrieved from https://www.verywellmind.com/mindfulness-the-health-and-stress-relief-benefits-3145189

Scott, E. (2022b). *How to reduce negative self-talk for a better life.* Verywell Mind. Retrieved from https://www.verywellmind.com/negative-self-talk-and-how-it-affects-us-4161304

Seppälä, E. (2021). *The power of self-compassion*. Ten Percent Happier. Retrieved from https://www.tenpercent.com/meditationweeklyblog/the-power-of-self-compassion

Seth, A. K. (2018). Consciousness: The last 50 years (and the next). *Brain and Neuroscience Advances, 2.* https://doi.org/10.1177/2398212818816019

Shethna, J. (2023). *Self-image*. EDUCBA. Retrieved from https://www.educba.com/self-image/

Siegel, D. J. (2007). *The mindful brain: Reflection and attunement in the cultivation of well-being*. New York: W. W. Norton & Company.

Smallwood, J., & Schooler, J. W. (2006). The restless mind. *Psychological Bulletin, 132*(6), 946–958. https://doi.org/10.1037/0033-2909.132.6.946

Stott, R. (2007). When head and heart do not agree: A theoretical and clinical analysis of rational-emotional dissociation (RED) in cognitive therapy. *Journal of Cognitive Psychotherapy, 21*(1), 37–50. https://doi.org/10.1891/088983907780493313

TEDx Talks (2016). *Psychology flexibility: How love turns pain into purpose | Stephen Hayes | TEDxUniversityofNevada*

[Video]. education. Retrieved from https://www.youtube.com/watch?v=o79_gmO5ppg

Thompson, R. A. (1994). Emotion regulation: A theme in search of definition. *Monographs of the Society for Research in Child Development, 59*(2-3), 25–52, 250–283. https://doi.org/10.2307/1166137

Trzesniewski, K. H., Donnellan, M. B., Robins, R. W. (2003). Stability of self-esteem across the life span. *Journal of Personality and Social Psychology, 84*(1), 205–220.

Turow, R. G. (2023). *Mindfulness, meditation and self-compassion – a clinical psychologist explains how these science-backed practices can improve mental health.* The Conversation. Retrieved from http://theconversation.com/mindfulness-meditation-and-self-compassion-a-clinical-psychologist-explains-how-these-science-backed-practices-can-improve-mental-health-198731

Valerio, S. (2019). *Section 2: What philosophy says about the self.* Understanding the Self (GED101) Digital Portfolio. Retrieved from https://utsged101portfolio.wordpress.com/section-2-what-philosophy-says-about-the-self/

Van Edwards, V. (2021). *10 powerful tips you can use to practice self-compassion.* Science of People. Retrieved from https://www.scienceofpeople.com/self-compassion/

Verastegui, V. (n.d.). *4 steps to help you practice self-compassion with the RAIN technique*. Rumie. Retrieved from https://learn.rumie.org/jR/bytes/4-steps-to-help-you-practice-self-compassion-with-the-rain-technique/

WebMD Editorial Contributors (2021). *What to know about emotional health*. WebMD. Retrieved from https://www.webmd.com/balance/what-to-know-about-emotional-health

Whitney, S. (2021). *Mental health exercises aren't just for lockdown*. MyProtein. Retrieved from https://www.myprotein.co.in/blog/training/boost-your-mood-with-these-mindfulness-exercises/

Williams, J. A. (2023). *5 steps to reset your emotions and find inner peace*. Heartmanity's Blog. Retrieved from https://blog.heartmanity.com/blog/5-steps-to-reset-your-emotions-and-find-inner-peace/

Williams, N. (2023). *Self-love, self-compassion & self-care*. Nicola Williams. Retrieved from https://www.nicola-williams.com/themes/self-love-and-self-care

Wolff, C. (2016). *11 surprising everyday things that can have an effect on your mood.* Bustle. Retrieved from https://www.bustle.com/articles/155648-11-surprising-everyday-things-that-can-have-an-effect-on-your-mood

Further Reading

Dan Harris's story: https://www.abc.net.au/triplej/programs/hack/dan-harris-positive-psychology-search-for-happiness/12444208

Dan Harris's story: https://www.forbes.com/sites/bryanrobinson/2020/11/04/abc-news-anchor-dan-harris-on-how-meditation-changed-his-personal-life-and-built-a-new-business/?sh=f7760e136c29

Confidence: https://parade.com/989608/marynliles/confidence-quotes/

Depression: https://parade.com/946073/parade/depression-quotes/

Emotional health: https://www.goodreads.com/quotes/tag/emotional-health

Happiness: https://www.oprah.com/spirit/10-happiness-quotes-we-love/all

Self-compassion: https://jessicadimas.com/self-compassion-quotes/

Self-kindness: https://www.goodreads.com/quotes/tag/be-kind-to-yourself

www.ingramcontent.com/pod-product-compliance
Lightning Source LLC
Chambersburg PA
CBHW070656130626
46553CB00005B/1722